MW01034423

DEMOCRACY FROM THEN TO NOW

From the First Democratic Thoughts
in Ancient Greece to Democracy
Throughout the World Today

ERIC NILSEN

Copyright © 2022 - All rights reserved.

The contents of this book may not be reproduced, duplicated or transmitted without direct written permission from the author.

Under no circumstances will any legal responsibility or blame be held against the publisher for any reparation, damages, or monetary loss due to the information herein, either directly or indirectly.

Legal Notice:

This book is copyright protected. This is only for personal use. You cannot amend, distribute, sell, use, quote or paraphrase any part or the content within this book without the consent of the author.

Disclaimer Notice:

Please note the information contained within this document is for educational and entertainment purposes only. Every attempt has been made to provide accurate, up to date, and reliable complete information. No warranties of any kind are expressed or implied. Readers acknowledge that the author is not engaging in the rendering of legal, financial, medical or professional advice. The content of this book has been derived from various sources. Please consult a licensed professional before attempting any techniques outlined in this book.

By reading this document, the reader agrees that under no circumstances is the author responsible for any losses, direct or indirect, which are incurred as a result of the use of the information contained within this document, including, but not limited to, —errors, omissions, or inaccuracies.

FREE download

pdf version of the old classic

Democracy In America

by

Alexis de Toqueville

Volume 1 (of 2)

https://mailchi.mp/shopsterise/politics-and-society

Scan the QR code or visit the website above

Contents

Introduction

Have you ever wondered where democracy originated? The word "democracy" is rooted in the Greek language and combines the two words' *demos'* and *'kratos'*. Demos means a citizen living within a particular (city) state, while kratos refers to power or authority. Democracy is commonly associated with the endeavors of the ancient Greeks, whom 18th-century thinkers viewed as the forefathers of the Western political society. Although it may be challenging to hypothesize that these 18th-century thinkers could translate these democratic ideals of the ancient Greeks into the modern democratic institutions, we see numerous similarities between the contemporary democratic institutions and those prevalent in 6th century BCE Ancient Greece. This book seeks to explore the historical roots of democracy and analyze its evolution over the millenniums into where it stands today.

Which city can claim to be the World's oldest democracy? Ancient Athens, in particular, is viewed by several political historians as the so-called "birthplace of democracy". They attribute this analysis to several political institutions in Athens which were democratic in nature. These included a meritorious "lot system" used to select individuals for most public office positions. The rotation policy guaranteed that no individual could hold a single position more than once. Similarly, Athens harbored a highly effective judicial system, mainly composed of juries comprising ordinary citizens, and wielded a significant influence over the rest of the government institutions. However, perhaps the most democratic institution was the *Ecclesia*, a legislative assembly where most policy decisions were taken, and every male Athenian could participate in the voting process. When we speak about "*direct democracies*", ancient Athens served as an example of the most "direct democracies". Here, ordinary citizens could not only vote directly in the assembly but also serve on the juries as public administrators and in top financial positions.

But who was the first to develop democratic ideas? It is interesting to note that most of the political philosophy and the debates about an "ideal political system" began as early as the 6th century BCE, when the likes of Plato and Aristotle introduced their conceptions about an ideal state. Plato argued that "*philosopher kings*" who were equipped with actual knowledge rather than just opinions and did not merely legislate but rule at their own discretion were the ideal rulers of a state. However, Aristotle took a different *inductive approach* rather than his teacher Plato's idealistic *deductive approach*. He argued that any political system, whether democratic or not, had within itself its seeds of destruction, and any constitution, including dysfunctional ones, could be made more stable. Furthermore, Aristotle argued that the rule of law was a prerequisite for a state to be stable and effective. By the rule of law, he meant that the state's law ought to be supreme over all citizens of a country, state, or community, regardless of their socio-economic differences. The political works of both Plato and Aristotle have continued to serve as the cornerstone of most contemporary political philosophical works. While Plato's principle of justice serves as the grassroots of our modern concept of ethics, Aristotle's rule of law is essentially at the heart of every modern state's constitution. But how did these first democratic ideas evolve into the democracy we know today? To answer that question, we will study the history of events that have led us to where we are today.

Following the Greek period, the Romans replicated some of the Greek democratic institutions while introducing some of their own. For example, the Roman Republic established separate legislative assemblies - the *Centuriae Assembly* and the *Tribal Assembly*. While the former dealt primarily with matters related to defense and strategy, the latter was comprised of non-military civilian magistrates responsible for promulgating administration-related *legislations* while also acting as a court for serious offenses. The Roman Senate was another vital institution that served as an advisory council and passed decrees called the "senate's consulta". Although they did not have a legal force, they were usually obeyed in practice. Through these decrees, the senators directed the magistrates regarding important military-related affairs. The Roman Republic era is also renowned for being the first time an extensive legal code (the "Law of the Twelve Tables") was introduced. It dealt with a comprehensive range of legal issues, including judicial process, debt recovery, and inheritance rights.

Was democracy still relevant during the medieval age- a period which is otherwise commonly associated with the prevalence of feudalism? Several new democratic institutions sprouted throughout the world during this era, challenging the common hypothesis that democracy was utterly a product of the 18th and 19th-century "democratization" process. Among the most prominent examples of political institutions from the medieval era was the Germanic "Thing" (or assembly) prevalent in Germanic society during the Viking Age. The things comprised local citizens, chaired by a lawman, and served not only as legislative assemblies but also as centers for social and cultural activities. Moreover, they also acted as courts and provided arbitration to groups and individuals facing tribal feuds.

Similarly, the Witenagemot (the meeting of wise men) was an important political institution in Medieval Anglo-Saxon England. It was primarily a consultative assembly comprising the aristocratic class, both secular and ecclesiastical noblemen. Their primary duty was to counsel the king regarding important foreign and domestic issues. Were these medieval-age institutions any relevant to the democracy we know today? Although many political historians opine that most medieval era institutions had to be demolished or replaced to pave the way for modern democracy, we will explore how several institutions underwent a transformation process and became an essential part of modern democracy.

What did the British give to democracy? We will analyze the numerous political developments in England that served as seeds of what grew into the democracy we know today. Among the significant developments was the introduction of the Magna Carta in 1215 by King John of England. The Magna Carta led to the Divine Rights Theory of Kings being challenged for the first time, and it was maintained that no individual, including the king, was above the law. Moreover, while the Magna Carta introduced several legal principles such as Habeas Corpus, it introduced a range of freedoms and liberties, such as the right to life, liberty, and property. These values and ideals inspired various legislators and politicians, including the framers of the U.S. Constitution, who practically gave these principles a legal character. On the other hand, the Bill of Rights, which was introduced following the Glorious Revolution in 1689, came to serve as the foundational principle of the British Constitution and relieved Britain from the arbitrary rule of the monarchy while allowing a consultative democratic framework as the primary mechanism for the state's

4

administration. Finally, a system of parliamentary democracy was introduced where the Parliament was defined as the supreme legal authority in the United Kingdom.

So, when did democracy start in America? We will shed light on the historical roots of democracy in America and the democratization process following the independence in 1776. While most historians view the colonial era or War of Independence as the starting point for American democracy, we argue that its earliest roots could be sketched back to the thirteenth-century Iroquois Confederacy of indigenous tribes. As several political anthropologists have argued, it is here where the earliest concepts of federalism and separation of powers emerged. However, the most prominent "democratization" process did occur following the war of independence by the 13 colonies against the colonizing forces. The Declaration of Independence of 1776 asserted that "all men were created equal and endowed with certain inalienable rights". Moreover, to guarantee these rights, it was ascertained that establishing a new government that derived its power from the common public was necessary. If the government failed to provide these rights, the people had the right to bring in a new government. While the 13 states initially formed their own confederation, various hurdles such as the inability of individual states to raise money through taxes prompted these states to meet at the Philadelphia Convention in 1787 to meet these challenges by forging a "stronger union". Following the convention, the previous Articles of Confederation were replaced by the new American Constitution. The new Constitution resulted from evolution and prevailing contemporary political thought, and it was unique in several ways from that of its English counterpart. While it was decidedly "written" and "codified" compared to the British Constitution, it offered a presidential system of government and a stringent system of checks and balances. Moreover, in the Bill of Rights, the Constitution also guaranteed a range of fundamental rights for all individuals, such as life, liberty, property, religious freedom, and freedom of speech, amongst others.

Similarly, America's practical and political situation drove the establishment of a federal system of government, in contrast to Britain, Canada, or Australia. The realization of the practical necessity of this model emerged from the Philadelphia Convention, where the Great Compromise initiated a dual system of congressional representation. This realization came following a debate between Edmond Randolph of Virginia, a populous state, who proposed a bicameral legislature with membership proportional to each state's population, and William Paterson of New Jersey (a small state), who advocated for a single house with an equal representation for all states. The debate led to the idea of a dual system of congressional representation where the membership of the upper house would be based on equal representation for all states, while the lower house was to have *proportional representation*. This idea served as the grassroots of the emergence of a robust system of federalism in the United States.

So, what were the main development in the journey of democracy in the 20th century? We will provide a glimpse into the events of the 20th century, where democracy proved triumphant throughout the world. Moreover, we will analyze the rise of America not only as a major world power but also as a torchbearer of democracy. While the first and second world wars proved catastrophic in terms of human and financial losses worldwide, it is evident that democracy proved to be victorious. While the allied powers, except for the USSR, were mainly democratic nations, the new peacetime institutions such as the League of Nations and later the United Nations championed democratic norms and values globally. Besides the international events, America also saw some of the most watershed political events of its history during the century. While the prolonged civil rights movement successfully led to the ratification of various stringent anti-segregation laws, the feminist waves emancipated women in the socio-political realm by providing them the right to vote and equal opportunities at work.

So, where does democracy stand today? In the later part of the book, we seek to compare and contrast the extent to which democracy prevails in some major countries worldwide at the time of writing. Using the Economic Intelligence Unit's (EIU) Democracy Index as a yardstick, we analyze some of the countries considered 'fully democratic' - such as the Nordic Countries like Sweden and Denmark, and the United Kingdom - to name a few. Similarly, we offer insights into some countries where democracy may have taken a back seat in the recent past - with the United States and India serving as key cases in point. On the other hand, we also analyze some of the least democratic countries globally today and assess some of the reasons why these nations have chosen to retain their autocratic credentials. Some of the key examples of these states include China, Russia, and the Gulf countries such as Saudi Arabia and the United Arab Emirates. Finally, a significant subsection of this chapter discusses the case of Taiwan. This partially-recognized country was aristocratic at its advent but has gradually evolved into one of the most democratic countries in Asia.

What are the major challenges of democracy? While democracy has generally triumphed throughout the world in recent decades and become the modus-operandi for numerous nation-states, it is at the same time faced with a series of hurdles and challenges. We seek to analyze some of these specific challenges that have seemingly caused democracy to take a back seat. The most evident example of such is the rise of radical *right-wing* and *left-wing* populism across the globe. In addition, while America has recently faced a backlash to immigration and multiculturalism, which has for years served as the heart of its spirit of nationhood, anti-immigrant bias has also prevailed in the political scene across Europe, particularly in Greece and France.

Moreover, democracy also has to face several other institutional challenges, such as corruption and red-tapism in developing countries, and structural flaws such as gerrymandering and filibustering in the case of America. However, there are still hopes for betterment. In the last chapter, we argue that although democracy may have backtracked in various countries, including the United States, certain positive developments, such as the incumbent President Biden's administration's policies offer a ray of hope. Although multiple challenges exist regarding foreign and domestic policy, one ought to remain optimistic albeit cautious.

While by no means a comprehensive encyclopedia on democracy, the essential goal of this book is to provide a general glimpse of the idea of democracy and its evolution throughout history. It delves into the ancient roots of democracy, beginning as early as Ancient Greece and Ancient Rome. Then, it tracks its evolution during medieval Europe until the renaissance and the various political developments in Britain around this time. These served as a blow to monarchial rule and the Divine Rights Theory of Kings while giving birth to various democratic institutions and ideas such as the sovereignty of parliament. Besides a mere evolution and track-down of its history, the book also offers the readers an opportunity to reflect on the various challenges that democracy faces today. One of these challenges is populism, which threatens its very foundations.

Chapter One

Democracy in the Greek City States

Although Greek city-states are typically associated with the advent of democracy, the roots of democracy sketch back to as early as 1100 BC, when the ancient Phoenicians used "governing by assembly" to reach consensus on vital issues. The story of Wen Amon, an Egyptian trader who traveled north to the Phoenecian city of Byblos to engage in the lumber trade, is an important historical source. As he reached Byblos, Wen Amon's cargo ship was raided by pirates. Upon hearing this, the Phoenecian prince of Byblos called his *mw'dwt*, an ancient Semitic word referring to assembly, to reach a decision (Macalister, 1914). Although the details of this incident are irrelevant, it tells us that the ancient city of Byblos was ruled, in part, by a popular assembly - one of the earliest traces of democracy.

Similarly, various historians claim that the earliest roots of democracy may be found in the Indian "Republic" cities of *Sanghas* and *Ganas*, which existed in the 6th century BC and persisted until the 4th century BC. Although there is no pure evidence available for the period, a Greek historian Diodorus, who wrote two centuries after Alexander invaded India, vaguely mentions that two independent and democratic states existed in India (Muhlberger, 1998). The Gana was primarily ruled by a monarch, known by the name of *Raja*, and a deliberative assembly. This assembly occasionally met to discuss and provide suggestions on various state issues. The body also had a degree of judicial, financial, and administrative powers.

Sparta

Despite these early democratic ideas, the most prominent historical records of democracy date back to the Ancient Greek period. Greece was primarily a loose collection of independent city-states referred to as poleis in its earliest days. While most of these were *oligarchies*, democratic Athens is mostly compared to the prominent example of oligarchic Sparta. However, although Sparta was traditionally oligarchic, it still resembled democracy in various ways. For instance, it rejected private wealth as a primary social differentiator. Furthermore, the political power in the Spartan government was primarily divided among four bodies:

1. Two Spartan kings (*diarchy*)
2. *Gerousia* (Council of Elders including the two monarchs)
3. The *ephors* (representatives of Spartan citizens)
4. The *apella* (an assembly of Spartans)

While the two kings presided over the government simultaneously, they hailed from two different backgrounds. This arrangement meant that the system of dyarchy limited the executive's effective power as power was divided between the two. The judicial powers in Sparta were commonly shared between the kings and the members of the gerousia. These members had to be above the age of 60 and were elected for life. Although, in theory, any Spartan over the age of 60 could stand for elections, in practice, they were usually selected from a group of aristocratic families that possessed great wealth. Besides judicial powers, the council of elders was also equipped with the vital power of legislative initiative.

On the other hand, Apella, an important democratic institution, was the assembly of the common Spartans, who were above the age of 30, and were responsible for electing the members of the gerousia and the ephors. Apella could also accept or reject any policy proposals brought forward by the gerousia.

Lastly, the five ephors were primarily responsible for overseeing the actions of the kings and other public officials and, if required, deposing them. They could serve for one year and could not be re-elected for a second term. Moreover, the ephors also had significant influence over Sparta's foreign policy formation and served as an essential executive institution of the state. Their executive authority included full responsibility for the state's educational system, which was vital for maintaining an efficient Spartan army, amongst others. However, historians have raised questions about the competency of the ephors. For example, Aristotle noted that while they were a crucial executive body of the state, they were appointed from the whole social body. This situation resulted in incompetent men, who could easily be bribed, holding office.

The Spartan system of governance was designed by the prominent Greek politician Lycurgus. He is attributed to having brought about drastic political reforms following the revolt of helots in the late 7th century BC. To ward off another revolt by the helots, he devised a militarised communal system that made Sparta unique amongst other city-states in Greece. His reforms revolved mainly around three Spartan values: *equality* (amongst Spartans), military fitness, and austerity. The reforms brought about by Lycurgus were compiled as a list of rules referred to as the "Great Rhetra", making it the world's first written Constitution (Rhodes, 2007).

These reforms allowed Sparta to become a military superpower, and its political system grew to fame throughout Ancient Greece for its ability to ensure stability and progress. The concept of equality, in particular, played an essential role in Sparta, as Spartans began to refer to themselves as *Homoioi* - men of equal status. This equality was also predominant in the state's public educational system, where all Spartans, irrespective of their economic or social background, could receive the same education. This fact received universal admiration from historians and philosophers such as Plato and Aristotle. Similarly, the women in Sparta had access to a range of rights such as inheritance, property, and public education, making them stand out amongst women from other Greek city-states.

In general, the ordinary citizens of Sparta had the freedom to criticize their rulers as well as the ability to depose or exile them. However, although the Spartan political system comprised these vital democratic elements, two significant factors characterized Sparta as an oligarchy. The first factor was that the individual freedoms of Spartans were restricted. As a Greek historian, Plutarch suggests, "no man had the freedom to live as he wished", but instead, they lived as if they were a part of a "military camp" who were all engaged in serving their state. Secondly, it has been argued that the gerousia was the most dominant power group, who effectively had access to various tools of government.

Given Sparta's political stability and economic prosperity, there were no significant changes brought about to the Spartan Constitution, and thus most of the oligarchic elements persisted. Moreover, these oligarchic elements strengthened following the abundance of gold and silver in the aftermath of Spartan victories in the Persian Wars. On the other hand, the Persian Wars had caused Athens to become a dominant power in Greece, and disagreements between Sparta and Athens over dominance soon ensued. This disagreement bred several military conflicts between Sparta and Athens, called the Peloponnesian War, which resulted in Sparta being victorious. However, both states suffered enormously due to prolonged conflict, and soon afterward, Philip II of Macedon emerged victoriously and put a defeating blow to all city-states to his south.

Athens

Historians often regard Athens as the birthplace of democracy, and as such, it remains an important starting point for democratic inquiry. The academic literature available about Athenian democracy is wide-ranging and spans over millenniums - starting from the works of Plato and Aristotle to Machiavelli.

Like most other Greek poleis, Athens primarily emerged in the 7th century BCE with a group of powerful elites. However, the poor policies of the *aristocracy* caused severe economic exploitation of the masses, alongside various other social and political problems. As these problems worsened during the 6th century BC, the masses engaged in a widespread revolt against the city's notables, as revolutions had become more prominent in the Greek world during the era. In Sparta, the constitutional reforms brought about by Lycurgus satisfied the whims of most citizens. On the other hand, in Athens, following a prolonged clash between the ordinary citizens and the city's wealthy elites, the locals turned to the politician Solon to mediate between the two rival groups and propose a viable solution to their problems.

Contributions of Solon to democracy

Solon was a prominent Athenian poet and lawmaker who Plutarch regarded as one of the ancient world's *Seven Wise Men*. He attempted to strike a balance between the whims of the public who felt oppressed, and the perks and privileges of the wealthy elite, by introducing a more equitable law code. Solon dichotomized the Athenian citizenry into four main economic classes, assigning different rights and duties to each. Similarly, he provided a formal composition and functions of various governmental bodies. Following his recommendations, every male Athenian citizen was given the right to attend the deliberative assembly (*Ecclesia*) and also the right to vote. The Ecclesia soon became the governmental body chiefly mandated to pass legislation and orders, elect public officials, and decide on appeals from the courts. In 594 BCE, Solon provided Athens with its first constitution through his wide-ranging political reforms. This constitution saved the state from an ensuing political, economic, and social decline. While some of his reforms proved unsuccessful, Solon is widely acknowledged for laying the foundations for Athenian Democracy.

Role of Cleisthenes, Ephialtes, and Pericles

Solon's constitutional reforms had proven successful in improving the overall economic situation of the Athenian marginalized classes. However, it could not do much to eradicate the intense political competition amongst the elite to control the archonship, the top executive position. As such, Peisistratus became the tyrant of Athens in 561 BCE and held power for over three decades until his death in 527 BCE. Following the collapse of tyranny in 510 BCE, the prominent lawmaker Cleisthenes proposed a complete overhaul of the current system of government, which the Ecclesia accepted. Cleisthenes restructured the Athenian citizenry into ten tribes to shift the foundation of the political organization away from familial loyalty and towards a political one and enhance the army's organization. Moreover, he also established the notion of isonomia (equality of rights for all male citizens) by granting more citizens access to authority. It was during this time the Athenians began to use the term "democracy" ("rule by the people") to describe their political system. These political developments assisted Athens in soon entering its "Golden Age", which was defined by its significant literary and artistic progress. Following the Persian Wars from 499 BCE to 449 BCE, the citizens from the lower classes who had participated in the military campaigns began to seek a more significant role in the administrative affairs of their city. Responding to their whims, Ephialtes and Pericles brought about a range of reforms aimed at uplifting the most oppressed segments of the Athenian society and providing them more access to political power. They shifted this power balance primarily by limiting the prerogatives of the Council Areopagus and allowing the *thetes* (poor Athenians) to hold public office. The most notable addition by Cleisthenes and Pericles to Athens' political and social scene was the notion of freedom and equality. Athenians now saw themselves as free citizens who were all equal regardless of the wealth they owned. Each individual now felt that they could participate in the political process which had previously been reserved for the affluent elites.

The Athenians appointed officials through the "lot" system to uphold these ideals. To guarantee that all people were "equally" eligible for service, casting lots were utilized, and allotment machines were used to eliminate corruption. Furthermore, for most positions chosen through this system, Athenians could not be selected for a single post more than once. This rotation policy

limited terms

helped assure that no single official built up a power base by holding a particular position for a prolonged period.

Another major political institution in Athens was the judiciary. The courts were primarily comprised not of judges but a large number of juries, who were selected by lot on a daily basis from an annual pool of individuals. The courts wielded a significant influence over the rest of the governmental institutions and their officials and could depose them whenever they deemed appropriate. Moreover, it was mandatory for the citizens who were a part of the jury to attend court proceedings. Furthermore, they were also provided financial compensation for doing so.

Elections were only conducted for the induction of the *strategoi* (military generals), which required strategic skills, and the treasurers, who had to be affluent since any misappropriated funds of the government had to be recovered from their personal wealth. At the Ecclesia, all Athenian male citizens could vote for significant policy decisions that required a majority vote. Following the vote, all policy decisions taken at the Ecclesia were carried out by the *Boule* of 500, a council of 500 public officials appointed to look after the daily administration of the city. The officials for the Boule were elected by lot annually, and no official could serve more than twice.

A general overview of the Athenian political system indicates that the system of democracy in place was "direct", but more direct than most direct democracies in the contemporary world. Athenian citizens could not only vote directly in the assembly but also serve on the jury as boule officials and top financial positions. Moreover, although the principles of equality and freedom, which are much-cherished today, were not guaranteed by some form of a written constitution, they still lay at the heart of the Athenian political system.

Chapter Two

The Greek Philosophers

"The state comes into existence so that men may live;
it remains in being so that they may live well."
—Aristotle (Politics 1:2)

The political developments across the Greek world, particularly the emergence of the Athenian democracy, prompted numerous philosophers to formulate their own distinct political theories. Amongst the first philosophers was Socrates (470-399 BCE), who sought to address the question of an individual's position within a community. However, most of Socrates' ideas were conveyed through Plato's written works.

Plato

Plato (427-347 BCE) is one of the most well-known and frequently read and studied Greek philosophers. Plato authored three large-scale political works: the Republic, Politicus or Statesman, and Laws. Although there is some disagreement about which of Plato's works is authentic, it is in the Republic that his political ideology receives the most influential exposition. In his works, Plato synthesizes political philosophy, metaphysics, and ethics into an interdisciplinary and well-structured philosophy. Plato's philosophical works rely almost exclusively on ideas presented by someone else. These are known as 'dialogues,' which are recordings of real and imagined talks between groups of individuals, with Socrates being the main protagonist.

Justice is one of the topics elaborately addressed by Plato in his works. In the Republic, Socrates is challenged on the issue of dikaiosyne (justice) by the 'radical' Sophist Thrasymachus (Reeve, 2004). Justice, according to Thrasymachus, is nothing but the self-interest of the stronger. This statement does not mean that justice is in the interests of the stronger, but that it is in the interests of the stronger for others to be just while he is unjust. His position can be summed up in four assertions:

1. The good life consists in ignoring all limits and restrictions and living a life of limitless gratification.
2. 'Justice' means 'compliance with the law,' so accept the limitations or controls imposed by a superior.
3. Laws are rules created by the powerful and imposed on the weak to control them to the advantage of the people in power.
4. The ruler's interests are thus best served when his subjects are just, and he can be unjust.

As such, Thrasymachus admires tyranny. Plato attributes this attitude to the erratic and violent style of politics he witnessed as a child and uses Socrates as a mouthpiece to refute it in The Republic. Thrasymachus believes that injustice is preferable to justice because justice entails accepting limitations. In his opinion, a just man is a kind of amiable fool. The naturally superior man understands that living a good life entails disregarding restrictions. However, on the other hand, Socrates points out that characterizing the good life in this way is a mistake. Musicians, physicians, and robbers all require some form of 'justice.' He asserts that 'justice' is natural because it is necessary for any coherent action and that injustice is not so much wrong as it is self-defeating. Justice is to a person what sharpness is to a knife, or curiosity is to the eye. It is the 'virtue' that allows the soul to function correctly. To understand what justice to the soul entails, one must first understand justice in the polis or state. We will appreciate justice on a small/individual scale if we consider it on a large scale.

Socrates addresses the question of "what constitutes the justice of the state" by describing the development of an illusionary 'ideal' state he calls Kallipolis ('Beautiful City'). He asserts that the state would emerge due to the need for humans to collaborate to meet material needs, the fulfillment of which would result in more sophisticated needs and the development of more complex structures to meet them. The state would have three occupation groups at the end of its evolution, among whom the state's 'virtues' would be distributed:

1. Guardians - embody the state's wisdom.
2. Auxiliaries or military class - exemplify bravery.
3. Producers - demonstrate prohibition or self-restraint and recognize the need to accept the guardians' rule.

Socrates suggests that justice is not a separate virtue in addition to bravery, wisdom, and self-restraint, but rather the relationship that exists when the Auxiliaries and Producers remain within limits prescribed by the Guardians. In other words, justice is obtained when the Guardians, Auxiliaries, and Producers work together to secure the good of the entire community. Justice entails everyone doing their job to the best of their abilities while not interfering with anyone else.

As Socrates claims, the state's justice is dependent on each class and each individual in the state conducting their respective duties appropriately. He further argues that, similarly, the justice of the individual requires that each of the three elements (namely reason, spirit, and appetite) in the individual soul are kept within their acceptable boundaries. Furthermore, he contends that none of the three can work adequately without the assistance of the others; hence a synergy amongst the three is necessary.

Plato is also well-known for his profound insights into education and why it is critical for the smooth functioning of a state. In his works, Socrates claims that we live in a world where certainty is impossible since no single perspective can be proven more valid than its opposite one. He claims that the world of ordinary sense experience is full of doubt, and that there is no guarantee that what we have experienced is actually true. However, he argues that the appropriate type of *education*, a philosophical education, can move the mind away from the tangible world of appearance and into a 'real' world of 'forms' or 'ideas'. He argues that any righteous action or a beautiful thing is only righteous and beautiful because it 'participates' in a pure idea of justice and beauty. He claims this is an idea that only an educated mind can comprehend. According to him, many things in the 'world of sight' exhibit ambivalence because they are merely imperfect representations or "copies" of the ideas they participate in. Most individuals only encounter copies without recognizing they are copies, mistaking appearance for reality. On the other hand, a philosopher has well-comprehended ideas themselves and whose action is therefore now informed by real knowledge rather than volatile opinions. He is a 'wisdom lover' rather than a 'lover of sights and sound'.

Plato can be viewed as a strong opponent of democracy. He claims that it fosters a society with no definite knowledge but just scattered opinions or beliefs that can be readily modified. Plato argues that democracies are unfavorable because their living conditions breed weak-willed and indecisive individuals. Instead, he proposes that philosopher kings rule a state since they are the only truly just men who have actual knowledge rather than just opinion. He suggests that the philosopher kings not merely legislate but rule at their own discretion. However, contrary to the popular belief of the Sophists, they will not exploit their citizens to further their own interests.

Although Plato's political philosophy is nuanced and thoughtful in several regards, it has been the subject of much criticism. For example, critics assert that Plato's philosopher kings reign over a totalitarian government. They are, in fact, similar to dictators who control every aspect of their citizens' lives based on their knowledge (Brown, 1998). They have also critiqued his theory of education, asserting that the type of knowledge Plato values does not liberate individuals but instead creates the kind of unfreedom he considers innocuous. Similarly, Plato defines justice as non-intervention between classes. Still, critics argue it is impossible for the ruling class not to intervene in the affairs of other classes because governing implies regulation, which is synonymous with interference. Furthermore, in his Theory of Justice, he classifies the state into three classes, which opponents argue is inapplicable to a modern nation-state characterized by many interests and segments. In reality, his classification of society into three classes, each with its own set of functions, leads to class privileges and elitism.

Some opponents have also suggested that Plato's political philosophy is remarkably similar to Modern Fascist ideologies. For example, they argue that similar to how fascism advocates the dictatorship of the Fascist Party Leader, Plato supported the dictatorship of the philosopher kings. In a similar vein, Fascism advocates for the rule of the Fascist intellect and the minority rule of the Fascist Party, similar to how Plato supported the rule of the intellect and regarded the minority rule of the guardians to be the finest of practical forms of government. Moreover, they also contend that Plato's Ideal State and the Fascist State are totalitarian in nature, regulating every element of the citizen and community's existence.

However, Platonists reject these criticisms on various accounts' arguing that his philosophical contributions, particularly his Theory of Justice and education, helped put politics on the right track. Firstly, they argue that criticizing Plato for not possessing the ideals, opinions, and ideas that current liberals appreciate is futile and that such criticism ignores Plato's real intentions. They argue that Plato is earnest in his view that a system of philosopher kings would not be in place for the rulers' advantage but for the sake of the collective and long-term welfare of all citizens of a state as a whole. He expects the philosopher kings to live austerity lives and devote their vast intellectual resources to society's wellbeing.

Similarly, they reject the premise that Plato's philosophy was, in any respect, fascist. Instead, they argue that Plato was anti-imperialism and thought and wrote in terms of the city-state, but fascism is imperialistic. They also suggest that Platonism is founded on political idealism and subordinates Politics to Ethics, whereas fascism is based on political realism and subordinates Ethics to Politics.

Considering the above, Plato may not be considered a proponent of democracy in the modern democratic sense. However, it could be argued that his real intention was the harboring of a society that had a political system based on a division of labor, justice, ethics, and communal welfare. The four values that serve as fundamental principles of democracy today.

Aristotle

Aristotle was the second most prominent Greek political philosopher after Plato, who made several contributions to political theory and whose works are still well-read throughout the world today. Aristotle is considered one of the greatest followers of Plato and received much of his inspiration from him. However, the two political philosophers had several fundamental differences. If Plato was a radical thinker, Aristotle's political theory was conservative. While Plato followed the *deductive method* of reasoning, Aristotle was decidedly an inductive thinker. Aristotle argued inductively by making comparisons of the functioning of a vast number of city-states that existed in his time and tested the validity of his hypotheses by referring to existing contemporary institutions.

In contrast, Plato deduced his ideal state based on certain assumed principles, such as the rule of philosophy, regardless of practical difficulties. Aristotle saw himself as a systematizer of existing knowledge rather than a proponent of new philosophy. As a result, his thinking is less inventive and more rational and scientific than Plato's, and his theories and judgments are more realistic.

Aristotle's philosophy was deeply impacted by the demise of the city-state, which was giving way to the Imperial System in his earlier days. He was also heavily affected by contemporary Hellenic assumptions and ideas, such as the fundamental superiority of the Greek over the barbarian and the city-state over other forms of social organization. His two works, Politics and Nicomachean Ethics are his most famous political works. While the former revolves around a technical analysis of the different ways states could be organized, the latter includes the ethical premises behind this reasoning.

The Idea of Citizenship and State

In Book III of The Politics, Aristotle explains his concept of the citizen and the state (Stalley, 1998). He classifies the idea of citizenship into essential and non-essential characteristics. For Aristotle, the important attribute that a citizen must possess, is neither residence, descent, nor legal privilege. Instead, it is the performance of civic duties, not for a limited but for an indefinite period. He defines a citizen as someone who contributes to the judicial and the legislative process as a member of the government institution. Either or both of which are basic tenets of sovereignty. The fundamental prerequisite for citizenship, according to Aristotle, is the ability to rule and be ruled in turn.

For Aristotle, a state (*polis*) had significant importance since it guaranteed the following:

- The economic prerequisites of morality.
- It establishes the educational conditions for the growth and realization of moral virtue.
- Social preconditions of our ethical good.
- The polis is therefore a natural community as it meets all the needs, moral and material, attached to the natures of those who occupy it.
- If severed from the polis, human beings lose their identity.

Classification of Governments

Unlike Plato, Aristotle did not advocate for a single ideal constitution from which all others must devolve. He understood that governments have found several methods to organize themselves and that we must deal with what exists rather than what ought to exist. He argued that even the worst political arrangements could be modified and that what worked best for one state (polis) may not work for another.

His comparisons led to the broad conclusion that constitutional forms may be divided into three main classifications:

1. Rule by one
2. Rule by few
3. Rule by many

Aristotle further classifies the various types of government into two main categories, according to (1) the number of people who have or share sovereign authority and (2) the objectives that governments aim to accomplish. These classifications allow us to differentiate between pure government systems and those that are corrupt. The six types of governments are as follows:

Pure Form

- *Monarchy* – having wisdom and virtue as its guiding principles
- *Aristocracy* – based on a mixture of virtue and wealth
- *Polity* – representing martial virtues, while power rests with the middle-class people

Corrupt Form

- *Tyranny* – representing force, deceit, and selfishness
- *Oligarchy* – representing the greed for wealth
- *Democracy* – representing the principle of equality with power in the hands of the poor

Aristotle suggests that even defective or dysfunctional constitutions may be made more stable with fairness. The stability of a constitution can be ensured by balancing components of 'fewness' and 'manyness' so that as few individuals as possible are excluded or alienated. Oligarchies will be hostile to the poor, who are many. Democracies will be hostile to the wealthy, who are powerful. Consequently, oligarchies could safeguard themselves by granting as many individuals as possible a share of political authority.

Similarly, democracies could become more stable by adopting moderation in income distribution and satisfying the affluent with dignified and valuable positions. He further argued that the most stable constitution would be one in which a large middle class shares political power: a government that is neither of the affluent few nor of the propertyless majority but somewhere in the middle. Such a system would ensure that individuals belonging to the middle class are not rich enough to be despised but are not wealthy enough to wish to depose the affluent.

On Democracy

Aristotle did not hold the same anti-democratic views as Plato. For him, democracy is a system of governance in which free citizens have absolute authority. He felt that the virtue and ability of the entire community outweighed the virtue and talent of a small portion of the population. Even though the general populace is unaware of the complexities of administration, they have the good judgment to pick competent administrators and lawmakers and monitor any wrongdoing on their part. As such, he supported a nebulous form of democracy. While he vested the ultimate sovereignty authority in the citizenry at large, he proposed that only the most qualified citizens should be tasked with running the actual state machinery.

The Relevance of Aristotle's Political Thought in the Contemporary World

As Arthur Herman (2013) suggests, "The ancient Greek philosophers Plato and Aristotle may seem like the quintessential Dead White Males, but they're very much alive". Essentially, Plato and Aristotle laid the foundations of Western political thought, and their thoughts and ideas are prevalent in several manifestations today. While the two philosophers had two different perspectives on the same issues, their debate itself is what wields significant importance. As Plato suggested, every soul in the world has an internal desire to attain a greater, more spiritual truth, and education was one of the critical ways to attain this truth. Furthermore, he opined that the ideal rulers were equipped with more excellent knowledge and virtue and possessed a selfless demeanor. In every political system today, these are essential virtues that citizens want their leaders to have.

On the other hand, Aristotle was amongst the first thinkers to "systemize" the knowledge related to politics and classify different types of political systems: monarchy, aristocracy, and democracy. Moreover, being a realist, unlike his idealist teacher Plato, Aristotle suggested that any political system, regardless of its composition, could prove to be desirable for its citizens but had within itself its seeds of destruction. As such, he emphasized the notion of the rule of law and the overall subjective wellbeing of the citizens, which he proposed should be the primary fundamental goal of any state. Of course, different political systems exist today. For example, even reasonably well-functioning democratic countries (such as the United Kingdom and the United States) have a series of institutional differences. Nevertheless, what analysts look for today is governments' overall success in maintaining the rule of law and uplifting the subjective wellbeing of their citizens.

Chapter Three

Democracy in the Roman Republic

T he city of Rome was founded in c. 753 BCE when settlements sprouted near the Palatine Hill along the Tiber River in contemporary central Italy. The city's foundations were synchronous with the advent of the Roman Kingdom, under which the Roman citizens elected kings (or monarchs) to serve for their entire lifetime. In 509 BCE, however, the last Roman monarch was deposed, leading to the foundation of the Roman Republic. Although several critics suggest otherwise, the nascent Roman Republic's government essentially functioned as a representative democracy. Before the establishment of the Republic, only the wealthiest elite (the *Patricians*) could wield important political or religious positions. Every non-Patrician was considered a *Plebian* who was not eligible to hold any public office. However, the Plebians struggled for their political rights and gained political power with time.

During the earlier days of the Roman Republic, the struggle between plebians and patricians also resulted in the establishment of crucial new government offices and institutions and the adaptation of existing ones to meet the evolving demands of the state. The institution of the Senate, in particular, underwent significant change. Under the monarchy, the Senate functioned as an advisory body to the emperor. However, it was now mandated to counsel both the magistrates and the Roman citizens. Although in principle, the sovereignty belonged to the Roman public at large, and the Senate just provided counsel, the Senate exercised significant influence in actuality due to the overall prominence of its members. In addition, two new assemblies were introduced during the Roman Republic era, apart from the Senate. These were the *centuriate assembly* and the *tribal assembly*. The Centuriate Assembly primarily dealt with matters related to the military and strategy and was comprised of 193 military magistrates who wielded military prowess. The Tribal Assembly, on the other hand, was comprised of non-military civilian magistrates who usually consisted of 30 *curiae* (or local tribal groups) who were responsible for bringing out essential legislations and acting as a court for serious offenses. However, although these assemblies were collectively accountable to the Roman citizens, the Senate continued to wield enormous powers as the elite patrician class dominated them.

Besides legislation, necessary legal reforms were also brought out during the Roman Republic. The first extensive written legal code, the Law of the Twelve Tables, was introduced in Rome in 451 BCE and was engraved on twelve bronze tablets and available for public display. The code addressed various issues, including judicial process, debt recovery, parental obligations, land rights, inheritance, and burial procedures.

As a result of these institutional reforms that resulted in economic prosperity and an increase in population, the Roman Republic was able to expand its territory and influence by the end of the 5th century BCE. While it initially captured Fidenae (437 BCE), a town near Rome, the territorial conquests continued for centuries, with the Republic emerging victorious in the Latin War (340 BCE to 338 BCE), Pyrrhic War (280 BCE to 275 BCE), and the Punic Wars (264 BCE to 146 BCE), to name a few. These conquests allowed the Republic to expand its territories from Syria and Egypt to Carthago Nova (present-day Spain) and Carthage (present-day Tunisia).

However, the rise in military expenditure came at the cost of domestic prosperity, as the Roman common middle-class soon began to feel the economic consequences. The farmers, who had to migrate to the cities since they could not raise crops and compete economically, were particularly affected. Similarly, while the aristocracy enjoyed the fruits of slavery, this proved disastrous for ordinary citizens. As a result of these developments, the Roman Republic was soon embroiled in endless civil wars, eventually transitioning from a republic into an empire.

The Legacy of the Roman Republic

Following the overthrow of the last monarch, the Etruscans, the Romans had established a 'republic'. This establishment essentially refers to a system of governance under which all citizens are expected to play an active role in governing the state. The political model adopted by the Roman Republic has continued to wield a tremendous influence on several countries for centuries. By and large, this model has been able to assist states in establishing a sustainable and robust democracy. For example, when one of America's founding fathers, Alexander Hamilton, argued for the ratification of the U.S. Constitution, he idealized the Roman Republic, stating it had "attained to the utmost height of human greatness" (Brown, 2016). Similarly, leaders such as Thomas Jefferson and James Madison studied the Roman historian Polybius, who provided one of the most detailed descriptions of the Roman Republic's Constitution.

Here members of different political factions and socioeconomic groups checked the power of the elites and the mob.

The institutions founded during the Roman Republic era, such as the Senate, have been adopted by many countries worldwide. However, the death of the Republic also serves as an important lesson for democracies today. The most severe threat that the Roman Republic faced was not the emergence of an ambitious tyrant but the gradual erosion of its cultural and political institutions. This degeneration began due to increasing economic disparities during the second century BCE. According to Watts (2021), similarly, the United States is also contemporarily faced with the emergence of a large gap between the haves and have-nots. While the Roman elites benefitted the most from the wealth plundered from the new provinces, the middle class failed to maintain their living standards. Although the Roman politicians sought to address these growing concerns by introducing various political reforms to enhance the equitable distribution of wealth, the failure to pass these reforms furthered the public's angst, leading to political violence for over 300 years, eventually resulting in the displacement of the Republic. Today's challenge for democracies such as the United States is much more significant than the mere election of a despotic president. The real challenge is the deterioration of their masses' economic and social conditions. By taking the fate of the Roman Republic as a case in point, the ideal way for countries to sustain their democratic institutions and systems is to ensure the welfare of their citizens and proactively address any socioeconomic concerns through effective policy-making and legislation.

Chapter Four

Evolution of Democracy in the Medieval Era

A lthough the Medieval Era is commonly known for the emergence and prevalence of feudalism, this hypothesis may be far from correct. The medieval ages began immediately following the fall of the Roman Empire in the 5th century and continued until the Renaissance period and the Age of Discovery in the late 15th century. This period was marked by population decline, the collapse of centralized authority, and mass migrations due to continuous invasions. During this time, the large-scale migrations included Germanic peoples, who formed new kingdoms in areas previously under Roman control. Similarly, the Umayyad Caliphate came into existence in the 7th century in North Africa and the Middle East, areas that were once under Byzantine control.

A great majority of modern democratic practices date back to the medieval era. Many societies during the middle ages had followed different institutional procedures to choose their leaders.

However, these practices were not primarily aimed at maintaining a democracy. Most of the states where these practices were followed were narrow oligarchies, such as Venice, or *absolute monarchies*, such as Florence, although a few *guided democracies* did exist.

Here is an overview of some of the fundamental democratic institutions established during the medieval period.

Germanic Thing

A thing (or "assembly") was a legislative assembly prevalent in the ancient Germanic society during the Viking Age (793 AD to 1066 AD). It was comprised of local citizens and chaired by a lawman. The thing did not meet at prescribed set intervals or a specific place but was held at different locations that were easily accessible for attendees. These assemblies were purposed to address legislative issues, serve as social events, and provide opportunities for trade and commerce.

Regarding their actual intended motive, the things served as both legislative assemblies and courts to make important political decisions at different levels of the society, local, regional and supra-regional. The Norwegian Law of Gulathing stated that only free individuals (not enslaved people) could participate in the assembly proceedings. Various sources suggest that women were also allowed to participate in the proceedings at the thing.

A significant factor that led to the things being set up was the continuous tribal feuding preeminent in the Scandinavian society. The tribal traditions had granted individuals the freedom to avenge the injuries or death inflicted on their relatives, leading to social disorder. As such, things were established to reduce tribal feuds by serving as a more authentic source of conflict resolution.

Besides conflict resolution, the thing also selected top public officials, including the kings and tribal chiefs. While the assemblies were not democratic in the contemporary sense of an elected parliament, they were established on the principles of impartiality and inclusion, effectively expressing the views of a wider group of individuals.

According to historian Torgrim Titlestad (2020), the ancient sites in Norway demonstrated a sophisticated political structure over a thousand years ago, characterized by solid attendance and democratic ideas. While the things also functioned as courts of law, and if one of the smaller things could not reach an agreement, the issue would be taken to one of the larger things, which covered a more significant area, a system similar to the modern-day concept of appellative courts. The Norwegian legislature is still known as the Storting (Big Thing).

The Witenagemot (folkmoot) of Early Medieval England

The Witenagemot (the meeting of wise men) was a prominent political institution in existence in Anglo-Saxon England from the 7th century until the 11th century. The Witenagemot was primarily a consultative assembly comprising the aristocratic ruling class (both secular and ecclesiastical noblemen and clergy). Their primary duty was to advise the monarch regarding important domestic and foreign issues. They counseled the king on administrative and organizational issues such as taxation, jurisprudence, and internal security on the domestic front. Regarding foreign matters, the advice was about defense issues such as the Norse invasions and the Norman Conquest.

Although the institution of Witenagemot was significantly different from the future Parliament of England, it served as a source of inspiration for the latter's formation, particularly concerning the constitution of the House of Lords.

Tynwald (Isle of Man)

The Tynwald on the Isle of Man was established over 1000 years ago and is considered one of the world's most ancient and continuous legislative institutions. The institution primarily has legislative and judicial functions, as it is responsible for promulgating laws and addressing petitions.

The Tynwald was initially composed of 24 members of the House of Keys, comprising four members from each of the six headings of the country. It is comprised of two chambers (also called the branches of Tynwald) which include the House of Keys (which consists of directly elected members) and the Legislative Council (indirectly chosen delegates). The Tynwald meets annually on July 5, Tynwald Day. The members were not initially elected using a vote but were selected for life, and their office was passed on through a hereditary process. Moreover, the Tynwald did not have regular sessions but met when required. The Keys resembled a jury and were occasionally brought to the session by the Lord of Mann when legal counsel was needed.

The Túatha System (Medieval Ireland)

The *Túath* (plural Túatha) was the primary political and legislative institution in Medieval-era Ireland. According to ancient Irish terms, a household comprised of about 30 individuals per dwelling. A *trícha cét* consisted of about 100 dwellings, and a túath was comprised of a group of tricha céta which made up about 9,000 individuals.

Each tuath had a tribal outlook and had its own executive, legislative, judicial, and defense system. The multiple tuaths allied together to form a confederation meant for mutual defense. The confederation was organized along hierarchical lines depending on geographical and social factors. Following the Elizabethan conquest, the previous Irish political and social setup was replaced by a system of baronies and counties. As a result of reforms during colonial rule, it is challenging to ascertain the exact organization and powers wielded by the *Túaths*. However, according to available literature, the tuaths served as a source of defense for the Irish people in the absence of a system of nation-states.

The Papal Election of 1061

Following the death of Pope Nicholas II in 1061, an election was held to elect a new Pope. This event was the first of its kind in the history of the Catholic Church. The six cardinal bishops decided to conduct an election, where they would serve as electors, eventually electing Anselmo de Baggio of Lucca (Alexander II) as the new Pope. This pioneer occasion ensured unanimity and impartiality in the selection process of a religious head.

Guild Democracies of the City-States

Various medieval-era city-states such as Venice and Florence in Italy and others in Switzerland had introduced a guild democratic system instead of a modern one. These democracies were essentially based on "lobby war" and had no institutional guarantees, such as the separation of powers. However, these states continued to evolve into oligarchies (such as Venice) or "Signories" with time. Although these *guild democracies* were not as democratic as the Athenian democracy, they served as significant instances of the evolution and development of democracy during the medieval era.

The Polish Wiec

The medieval era Slavic countries such as Poland, Novgorod, and Pskov had a system of popular assemblies known as the *Wiec* or *Veche*. The veche was similar to the Germanic thing or the Swiss *Landsgemeinde*. The word Wiec is rooted in the Proto-Slavonic word *vetje* (literally meaning 'counsel' or 'talk'). The Wiec in Poland is known to have evolved into the *Sejm* (contemporary Polish Parliament) in 1182. In the case of the Republic of Novgorod, the veche severed as the supreme legislature and judicial authority until the conquest by Grand Prince Ivan III in 1478. Scholars argue that various reforms in 1410 allowed the Veche in Novgorod into an institution similar to the legislative assembly of Venice.

Sketching Democratisation to the Medieval Era

Amongst most modern political theorists, there appears to be a general consensus that the current democratization process mainly occurred in the 19th and 20th centuries. There is also a general agreement that it required the removal of various medieval institutions. They often quote Karl Marx, who famously remarked that the "medieval trash had to be swept away" (Møller, 2015) to allow modern representative democracy to flourish. These scholars rightly point out that several medieval institutions had to be replaced to pave the way for modern bureaucratic institutions - particularly institutions of local government, and various privileges for elite groups such as tax exemptions. Therefore, as Møller argues, various medieval institutions required transformation. However, these institutions also positively affected the bureaucratization and democratization processes in the 19th and 20th centuries. For instance, different social groups with political power restrained a top-down state-building approach, making the authoritarian rule more difficult. The Tuaths in medieval Ireland, for example, were comprised of diverse groups of people and confederated for shared political and social goals such as defense. In such localized institutions, it was difficult for a single individual to establish control over a state single-handedly. As Møller suggests, several medieval-era institutions served as "transmission belts" for the modern state-building process. This allowed a diverse range of social groups to be included in the democratization and bureaucratization process. This inclusion depended on their social standing and bureaucratic expertise, amongst others.

Chapter Five

The Divine Right of Kings, Magna Carta and the Glorious Revolution

The English Parliament was the most influential assembly in Europe founded during the Middle Ages in terms of the development of representative democracy. The parliament arose from the kings' councils, which were convened to redress grievances and exercise judicial functions. It came into formation more as a result of evolution rather than being a product of design. Gradually, the parliament began to deal with significant issues of public interest - most typically the collection of revenues required to fund the policies of the monarch. It predominantly became a legislative body, as a result of most of its judicial powers being delegated to courts. By the late 1600s, the English political system had become what could be characterized as a modern parliamentary system. The ratification of any law required the approval of both houses of Parliament; the House of Commons and the House of Lords. However, the evolution of the English Parliament resulted from a series of reforms throughout the Medieval Ages.

The English political system was mainly dominated by monarchs who wielded great near-absolute control over political, legislative, and social matters. What served as a significant turning point for the British political system was the Glorious Revolution of 1688-89. The Glorious Revolution refers to a series of events that involved the deposition of King James II of England by his daughter Mary II and her husband William III, the stadholder of the Netherlands. What had primarily led to the rebellion was the pro-Catholic policies that James II had introduced during his reign. He had overtly patronized Roman Catholicism which alienated most of the local Protestant community, as he introduced the Declaration of Indulgence in 1687. This declaration aimed to abolish all laws against the non-conformists and recusants - a step criticized by the British majority community at large. What further promoted the anguish against him was the birth of his first son to Mary of Modena, his Roman Catholic queen. Fearing the coronation of a Catholic monarch following his death, several prominent politicians from both the Whig and Tory parties wrote to William of Orange and requested him to intervene and resolve Britain's undue challenges.

One of the first challenges William had to face was the need to continue the government and convene the Parliament. Upon its assemblage, after engaging in a lengthy debate, the Convention Parliament decided that Jame's voluntary exile was similar to an abdication and offered the Crown jointly to William and Mary. However, the offer for William and Mary came with the condition that they would agree to the Declaration of Rights, which would later turn into the Bill of Rights. The latter would prove vital in giving Britain a more democratic and less monarchic outlook, laying the groundwork for the nation's political and economic development.

The Bill of Rights

The British Bill of Rights, formally "An Act Declaring the Rights and Liberties of the Subject and Settling the Succession of the Crown", was introduced in 1689. It was introduced following the deposition of King James II at the Glorious Revolution and the coronation of William and Mary as monarchs. The Bill of Rights was primarily developed from the Declaration of Rights and served as one of the foundational documents of the British Constitution. Before introducing the Bill of Rights, the Toleration Act (1689) had promised religious freedom to the Protestants, and the Triennial Act (1694) had introduced a system of general elections every three years. These were some of the policies that had been a major departure from the previous pro-Catholic and pro-absolutist policies of James II. Following the Glorious Revolution, the Bill of Rights had primarily aimed at providing the government with a democratic foundation on which it would continue to exist for centuries to come.

Although the Bill of Rights was generally not a product of innovation but merely declared the existing laws officially, the revolution settlement was a major departure from the previously established political norms. According to the settlement, the monarchy's powers were greatly reduced insofar that the monarchy and the decisions taken by the monarch had to be conditional on the will of the Parliament. These milestone steps relieved Britain from the arbitrary rule of the monarch and allowed a consultative democratic mechanism to assist the state's governance.

These developments served a crushing blow to the theory of the Divine Right of Kings, which had been the primary source of legitimacy for the British monarchs over the years. The view was based on the metaphysical idea that a king was pre-destined to be a king even before birth. Democratic ideas, such as liberty and equality, erupted during the Age of Enlightenment in the 17th and 18th centuries. These ideas served as an antithesis to the previous metaphysical ideas of a predetermined status. Perhaps the greatest challenge to the theory was the Glorious Revolution and the succeeding Bill of Rights, which helped abolish the absolutist monarchy in England and assisted in garnering world-view support in favor of democracy.

The Magna Carta

Although the Glorious Revolution and the following Bill of Rights helped establish democratic values and systems in Britain, the Magna Carta still serves as the most acknowledged first document of democratic rights in the world.

The Magna Carta Libertatum (Medieval Latin for "Great Charter of Freedoms") is primarily a royal charter of rights signed in 1215 by King John of England, much earlier than the glorious revolution. The Archbishop of Canterbury, Stephen Langton, initially devised it to make peace between the unpopular King and a group of rebel barons. It pledged to defend religious rights, safeguard barons from illegal detention, provide timely justice, and limit feudal payments to the Crown. A council of 25 barons would carry these out. However, the charter was revoked by Pope Innocent III during the same year because neither party kept its promises, resulting in the First Barons' War.

Although it was reinvoked by his successor son Henry III in 1216, it proved unsuccessful since the latter had removed some of the most fundamental aspects of the document to build his political base. However, by the end of the 16th century, the Magna Carta began to draw the interest of several academics, lawyers, and politicians who began to reconsider its worth during the changing circumstances. It was determined that the Magna Carta was very weighty to the British political system because it provided a series of religious rights and fundamental legal rights such as *habeas corpus*. Similarly, the Magna Carta served as the basis of the opposition to the divine right theory that had become predominant during the time, particularly following the Glorious Revolution.

The British Constitution

The English Constitution has been in the process of continuous transformation ever since the Norman Conquest. Following the period of consolidation came the emergence of the English Parliament. It was then followed by the English Parliament's efforts to restrain the king's powers. The struggle was long, but the English Parliament was eventually able to bring the king under its influence. The country's Cabinet system was developed in the following phase, which has continued unabated. However, unlike several other democracies worldwide, such as the United States, the United Kingdom has an "unwritten" rather than a written constitution.

According to Munro (1999), the English Constitution is "a complex amalgam of institutions, principles, and practices. It is a composite of charters and statutes, of judicial decisions, of common law, of precedence, usages, and tradition. It is not a single document, but many. It is not derived from a single source but from several. It is not a complete thing, but a thing which is still in the process of growth".

Many viewed the complexity of the constitution due to its loose nature as an unnecessary phenomenon. However, others attribute its nature to its success. According to J.G. Latham (1931), "The British Constitution has been a success largely because it has been loose and elastic and has left things to be determined by the common-sense of statesmen as emergencies arise, instead of being decided with the precision of lawyers in the interpretation of written documents."

The Constitution primarily references several statutes and conventions that serve as the official basis of the English legislative and administrative structure. The vagueness of the nature of the Constitution is perhaps best described by the American philosopher Tocqueville (1831), who suggests, "in England, the Constitution - there is no such thing. The English Constitution is not to be found in any one written document which can be conveniently referred to – the English Constitution does exist and can be studied both from conventions and its written elements".

As such, there are numerous sources of the English Constitution which include the following:

- Magna Carta
- Statutes
- Judicial decisions
- Common-Law
- Textbooks on Constitutional Law
- Royal Prerogatives
- Conventions

Here are some of the other salient features of the Constitution:

- Form of government: England is governed by a parliamentary system. The executive is accountable to the legislature, and only the party with a majority in Parliament forms the ministry. It remains in office as long as that confidence exists – if the ministry is defeated, it must resign. Ministers are held accountable to Parliament for their acts of omission and commission; governance is carried out following the democratic will of the people as expressed through their elected members in Parliament.

• Monarchy: England has a limited monarchy (or constitutional monarchy) which means that the powers of the king of England have gradually been eroded and are now exercised by ministers in the king's name. The king is powerless to act without the advice and consent of the ministry.

• Supremacy of British Parliament: The British Parliament enjoys control over all issues of public importance. Munro suggests, "the one thing it cannot do is to bind its successors. It cannot interrupt or put an end to the process of constitutional change."

• Its unreality: Nothing in it is what it appears to be or appears to be what it is. England has a king, but he has no real power. We talk about Parliament's sovereignty, but the Cabinet holds the real power.

• The rule of law: The supremacy of law presupposes that no individual is subjected to arbitrary punishment. No one is above the law, including the highest public officials.

• Judge-made constitution: The majority of the rights enjoyed by English citizens are guaranteed by judicial decisions issued from time to time.

• Principle of checks and balances: There are various checks and balances in play in the case of the British Political System prescribed by the constitution. For example, the two Houses can pass legislation, but it is only effective if signed by the king. Similarly, no king's order is valid unless and until a minister of the country countersigns it. Ministers in England are accountable to Parliament, which has the power to remove them through a vote of no-confidence. Similarly, the prime minister has the authority to request that the king dissolve parliament. The executive appoints judges, but the executive cannot remove them once appointed.

The Legacy and Relevance of the Magna Carta

The Magna Carta, which was introduced in Britain over 800 years ago, has arguably served as one of the greatest inspirations behind the 18th and 19th democratization processes in countries around the world. Firstly, the Magna Carta serves as a source of individual liberty. It granted several individual rights that were unfounded previously. One of the key clauses of the document stated that imprisonment of any individual must occur through a legal process. Clause 39, which is referred to as Habeas Corpus, suggested, "No free man shall be seized or imprisoned, or stripped of his rights or possessions, or outlawed or exiled, or deprived of his standing in any other way, nor will we proceed with force against him, or send others to do so, except by the lawful judgment of his equals or by the law of the land" (Hudson et al., 2015). The concept of Habeas Corpus established the notion of the rule of law, shielding ordinary citizens from any arbitrary punishments which were otherwise common.

Therefore, the Magna Carta initiated the concepts of the rule of law and equality before the law, which began to serve as the cornerstones of most human rights declarations and state constitutions. Examples included the Bill of Rights in Britain (1689), the Declaration of the Rights of Man and the Citizen in France (1789), and most significantly, the Bill of Rights in the United States (1791). As political expert Kaminski (1991) suggests, "For early Americans, Magna Carta and the Declaration of Independence were verbal representations of liberty and what government should be—protecting people rather than oppressing them."

For the American democracy, the most relevant classes of the Magna Carta were those that guaranteed the right to a trial by jury, protection against excessive punishments, and the safeguard of individual liberty and property. While writing the Federalist Papers, James Madison (1787) particularly referred to the 40th clause of the Magna Carta as he wrote, "Justice is the end of government. It is the end of civil society. It ever has been and ever will be pursued until it be obtained, or until liberty be lost in the pursuit".

Besides the American democracy, the Magna Carta also influenced the political developments of the 20th century when it influenced the Universal Declaration of Human Rights (UDHR). UDHR was adopted in 1948 and signed by a large number of countries around the world. Similarly, its principles also served as a fundamental inspiration for the European Convention on Human Rights in 1951. This convention has now been incorporated into British law.

The Magna Carta, introduced in Britain in 1215, has continued to serve as an inspiration for democratization and legalization processes throughout the world for centuries. Besides the principles of liberty, the rule of law, and accountability, the Magna Carta can also be viewed as a starting point for popular democracy and community engagement (Fisher, 2015). The principles essentially served as the grassroots for democracy and the demolishment of arbitrary and despotic rule worldwide.

Chapter Six

From Indigenous America to a "City on the Hill"

We the People of the United States, in order to form a more perfect Union, establish justice, insure domestic Tranquility, provide for the common defense, promote the general Welfare, and secure the Blessings of Liberty to ourselves and our Posterity, do ordain and establish this constitution for the United States of America. (The Preamble of the United States Constitution)

For most American historians, the starting point for America's democratic history is usually the colonial and post-colonial periods of the 17th and 18th centuries, particularly the American Revolution between 1765 and 1791. The political ideas that emerged from the European Age of Enlightenment and colonial rule shaped American politics in several regards. However, anthropologists argue that several ideas leading to the United States Constitution and American democracy are rooted back in the different indigenous peoples of the Americas.

While we traditionally tend to relate to indigenous people as hunter-gatherers, several groups established social and political institutions such as large-scale organized cities, city-states, and chiefdoms. The most prevalent system of government was in the case of the Iroquois Confederacy, a group of indigenous tribes that had a participatory democratic government with separate administrative, legislative, and judicial branches. The Iroquois Confederacy also had its own constitution, the "Great Law of Peace". The law was introduced following the confederacy's establishment in around 1450 by Dekanawidah and his spokesman Hiawatha and ratified by five tribes near modern-day Victor, New York. The Constitution comprised 118 articles, and each nation or tribe had its distinct role in the administration of the confederacy. While the Iroquois claim the events to have dated back to the late 12th century, some Western scholars suggest a later period of the 13th century.

Several historians, such as Grinde and Johnson (1991), have suggested that the political ideals of the Iroquois were of great inspiration to framers of the U.S. Constitution, including Benjamin Franklin and James Madison. They suggest that the framers proposed a federal structure for the United States after being inspired by the Iroquois confederation and the notions of liberty and the separation of powers.

Decolonization and the Independence

During the 17th and early 18th centuries, America was primarily a group of 13 British colonies. While the continent arguably became a "melting pot" of cultures and economic activity ushered during the period, the political scene was heavily dominated by Britain.

Following a rebellion against England, on July 4, 1776, 13 American colonies issued the "Declaration of Independence". They declared themselves free and proclaimed that they

> ...have full power to levy war, conclude peace, contract alliances, establish commerce, and do all other acts and things which independent states may of right do." They also asserted "that all men are created equal; that they are endowed with certain unalienable rights; and that to secure these rights, governments are instituted among men, deriving their just powers from the consent of the governed; and that whenever any form of government becomes destructive of these ends, it is the right of the people to alter or abolish it, and to institute a new government, laying its foundations on such principles, and organizing its powers in such manner; that whenever any form of government becomes destructive of these ends; it is the people's right to change or abolish it, and to establish a new government, based on such principles and organizing its powers in such a way that they believe will best ensure their safety and wellbeing. (Declaration of Independence, 1776)

The 13 states formed their *Confederation* on November 15, 1777. However, the confederation had various flaws, such as the inability to organize a military under such conditions in addition to the following four challenges:

1. the inability to raise money through taxes
2. the inability to borrow money
3. the inability to regulate commerce
4. the inability to provide adequately for the common defense by raising and supporting armies

Keeping these limitations in mind, representatives of these thirteen colonies decided to meet in Pennsylvania at the *Philadelphia Convention* in 1787, in a bid to not only tackle these challenges but form a stronger union and draft a new constitution. Given their extensive political experience and practical knowledge, Thomas Jefferson characterized the representatives as "an assembly of demigods". The convention successfully drafted a constitution for the United States and submitted the same to the states for approval. The previous legislative document, the Articles of Confederation, had proved to be weak, and the confederate states had operated like autonomous states. However, the new constitution was a departure from the former in several regards. The delegates had formulated a model for a stronger federal government that included three branches—executive, legislative, and judicial, as well as a system of checks and balances to ensure that no single unit would wield too much influence.

Salient Features of the American Constitution

As we have discussed earlier, the framers of the American Constitution were influenced by several political institutions and documents that had even predated the colonial period. For instance, the Magna Carta (1215) had served as the source of the principles of the rule of law, right to life, liberty, and property. Similarly, some of the political ideals of the Iroquois Confederacy, such as a federal system of government and separation of powers, found their way into the American Constitution. However, at the same time, the U.S. Constitution had several salient features, making it unique from most other states' constitutions.

To begin with, the U.S. Constitution is one of the briefest constitutions in the world, comprising just as many as seven articles. This is because the framers merely laid down the fundamentals and not the details. On the other hand, the framers also allowed other states which joined the federation to have their own constitutions as they had existed before. This allowance was made primarily to grant the federating states a sense of autonomy and avoid any fears of an oppressive central government.

Another salient feature of the U.S. Constitution was introducing a republic form of government. Every state was ensured protection against invasion and assistance against any domestic insurrection.

The preamble of the American Constitution is yet another highlight of the constitution. The framers deliberately used the phrase "We the people" to indicate the people's sovereignty. They had aspired to establish justice, ensure domestic tranquility, provide for the common defense, promote the general welfare, and secure the "blessings of liberty". While the constitution emphatically suggested that ultimate powers had to be vested in a large popular electorate, civilian supremacy had to be respected by the military, among other key state institutions.

The U.S. Constitution favored a representative form of democracy, where political institutions were to be run by public representatives, chosen directly or indirectly by them. However, on the other hand, democracy was "indirect" because voters could not initiate any federal laws or referendums, and this was up to their elected representatives or officials to decide. There were only three occasions on which voters could participate directly in federal affairs: when voting for the representative, when choosing the senators and when voting for electors to elect the president and vice-president.

Lastly, to preclude the exercise of arbitrary power by any political institution or person, the framers introduced an elaborate system of separation of powers, coupled with checks and balances. While Article 1 provided that all legislative powers granted shall be invested in Congress, Article 2 provided that the executive powers shall be vested in the president. According to Article 3, the judicial powers were to be vested in one Supreme Court and such inferior courts as the Congress may from time to time ordain and establish.

How the System of Separation of Powers Emerged

The system of separation of power was primarily meant to preclude the exercise of arbitrary power by dichotomizing the state's powers into three: the executive, the legislature, and the judiciary. Similarly, a bicameral system of congress was introduced to keep individual states from being overrun by more powerful ones. While the theory of separation of powers was proposed by the French philosopher Montesquieu and was also adopted earlier by the Iroquois Confederacy, the practical need for such a system primarily emerged when the constitution was being framed.

As the framers were working on the constitution, there was great jealousy among the states, which manifested itself in the debates regarding representation in the new Congress. The larger states with a larger population expressed concern that the new government would pass laws that were detrimental to their best interests. They feared that the numerous small states might pass laws harmful to the bigger states' best interests. To ensure protection against such legislation, Edmund Randolph of Virginia, a large state, suggested that representation in Congress be based solely on population. In contrast, William Patterson of New Jersey, a small state, proposed that representation be based on states rather than people, with each state being treated equally regardless of size. The dispute led to the *Great Compromise*, under which there would be two houses of Congress. In one house, seats would be divided among the states based on population, with the larger states having an advantage. In the second house, the states were to be represented equally, regardless of size, giving small states an advantage. According to the system, a bill must pass both Houses to become law, and each group of states has a veto over proposed legislation.

Important Conventions of U.S. Constitution

Party System – The constitution does not mention a party system, and its development is left to convention. According to George Washington, the American president must be a national leader who leads the country evenhandedly. However, he acknowledged that party considerations were prioritized in selecting his successor. On the one hand, under Alexander Hamilton, the Federalists advocated for the cause of industrialists, rich people, and the urban middle class. On the other, the Republicans under Thomas Jefferson supported rural folk, native farmers, etc.

Indirect election of the president – The American Constitution provided an indirect presidential election. The people would elect members of the Electoral College, who would then elect the president. However, as a result of convention, elections have become more direct. When candidates run for the Electoral College, they pledge to their political parties that if elected, they will support the party's candidate for the Presidency.

National Convention – Each political party holds its National convention approximately six months before the presidential election. The Convention nominates candidates for the office of president, but it is up to the president to select his running mate for vice president's office. The Convention also issues an election manifesto in which it appeals to electors to vote for its nominees as presidential electors.

Number of Electors – The constitution requires that every state shall designate, in the manner directed by its legislature, a number of electors equal to the total number of senators and members of the House of Representatives to which it is entitled. On the other hand, political parties nominate their respective candidates for electors through a convention. Every state has a tradition of awarding all electoral votes to the party that wins the state.

Messages of the President – At the start of each Congressional Session, the American president sends a message on the state of the Union. He lays out his administration's broad policies and asks Congress to pass the necessary laws and give him the authority to carry those policies out. Some of these messages have taken on historical significance. For example, in 1823, President Monroe enunciated "The Monroe Doctrine," one of the cardinal principles of American foreign policy, which aimed to warn the European powers not to oppress or control any country in the northern hemisphere. Similarly, President Eisenhower enunciated the famous "Eisenhower Doctrine" in his message to Congress in 1953, which laid out American foreign policy toward Middle Eastern countries.

Expensive and Exhaustive method of election – Ogden and Peterson (1968) point out that electing a president of the United States is "boisterous, expensive, exhaustive and contentious". Despite this, and according to a convention, as soon as it is clear who is winning the presidential election, the loser should be the first to send a congratulatory telegram to his winning opponent and offer full cooperation to the regime. This convention was set by the presidential candidate Barry Goldwater in 1964 when he congratulated President Johnson upon winning the election and offered him his full support. Similarly, according to another convention, the exiting president attends the swearing-in ceremony of the president-elect at the U.S. Capitol as a gesture of smooth transition of power. Such conventions are not standard in most parliamentary forms of government, where the leaders of the opposition work round the clock to destabilize the ruling party. However, only recently, both conventions were violated by Donald Trump, who refused to congratulate or attend president-elect Biden's oath-taking ceremony - a move criticized by many.

Senatorial Courtesy – When the president needs to make an appointment in a specific state, he must consult with the senators from that state who are members of his party. President Garfield was assassinated for violating this convention. Nevertheless, the convention is invariably followed, as it is in the president's interests to follow the convention. He can keep the senators in good humor and hope for their support and approval in matters of treaty ratification, etc.

Term for the presidential election – Another convention states that no president may run for re-election for a third time. President Washington convened the convention after refusing to run for re-election for a third term. However, President Roosevelt, who was elected for a fourth term, violated the convention (on account of World War II). The convention was replaced in 1951 by the 22nd amendment, which states explicitly that no American president may be elected a third time.

The constituency of the Representatives – another convention says the member of the House of Representatives must belong to the constituency from which he or she is returned.

Conduct of Work – procedure regarding the conduct of work of the House of Representatives is also based on convention.

Interviews with the media– weekly interviews by the president are given based on convention.

Steering Committee – The Steering Committee, majority floor leader, and Caucus are not recognized by the constitution but are established by convention.

Leader of the majority – according to another convention, the American Speaker is a party man and the leader of the majority in the House of Representatives.

Cabinet Members – According to convention, the president should appoint people from various states rather than just a few – introducing elements of Federation into his Cabinet.

Spoil System – When the president changed during the nineteenth century, so did the government's servants. As a result, the president had supporters in every office, and government business was conducted along partisan lines. This system resulted in corruption, inefficiency, and irresponsibility. However, the 1883 Pendleton Act established a system of competitive examinations for government office recruitment. The system eventually filled approximately 80% of government jobs. The spoil system has generally been replaced by a non-partisan merit system at the federal level.

Federal form of Government – Unlike Canada and Australia, the United States has a federal government. The states retain residuary powers, while the federal government has been given specific powers. As an initial result, the federal government was very weak, and the states were very strong. Due to such, the southern states were able to raise the standard of revolt against the federal government. As a result, the country experienced the Civil War between 1861 and 1865. However, various political scientists describe the country's federal structure as one of the key factors behind its unity and progress.

Basic Rights under U.S. Constitution

The Bill of Rights (1791), which refers to the first ten amendments of the American Constitution, serves as the cornerstone of the American ideals of democracy and the rule of law. A number of rights and protections are guaranteed under the Bill of Rights, ranging from freedom of speech and assembly to freedom from arbitrary detention.

The first amendment is perhaps the broadest and the most prominent of the Bill of Rights, as it guarantees many individual rights and liberties. Under this amendment, individuals are guaranteed freedom of speech and freedom of the press. Moreover, it is mandated that Congress must not make any law that supports the establishment of religion or prohibits the free exercise thereof. Other than this, individuals are given the right to assemble peacefully and petition the government to redress their various grievances.

The fourth through eighth amendments deal with several legal rights that serve as the sources of America's legal system. For example, according to the fourth amendment, individuals are given freedom from arbitrary searches and seizures, and it is provisioned that no warrants must be issued without any probable cause. Similarly, protections are provided against punishment for treason without trial, arbitrary arrest or detention (except in the case of rebellion or war), and the right of every individual to a fair trial.

The Bill of Rights affirms every individual's right to life, liberty, and property. In addition, all individuals are provided the right to vote regardless of their race, color or creed. Above all, all individuals are to be treated equally before the law.

The American "Exceptionalism"

Various political scientists and analysts have described the United States as inherently different from other nations. They argue that the country's values, political system, and historical development vastly differ from other countries, making it stand out as "exceptional". While the prevalent notion that these factors naturally entitle America to play a distinctive role on the world stage may be debatable, these scholars are accurate in their analysis of the country having a unique set of values, political system, and history.

In terms of its political system, several aspects of the American Constitution and the political system make it unique from most other countries worldwide. For instance, America was amongst the first countries to adopt a presidential system of government with a set of checks and balances. In the British parliamentary system, the prime minister and his cabinet are derived from the parliament and answer to it. In the United States, the president is elected by the voters separately from the members of Congress and is not directly accountable to congress. This system allows a more stable government and speedy decision-making as the president can respond to emerging situations with lesser constraints and legislative requirements for approval of his policies. However, one may argue that a presidential form of government could potentially increase the likelihood of authoritarianism in the case of a despotic president, as evidenced in the case of Donald Trump. In such situations, the system of checks and balances allows the legislature and the judiciary to keep a "check" on the president's ambitions and regressive policies through several ways, such as control over the budget, impeachment, and removal from office. Similarly, the judiciary can check on the president and congress' regressive policies through *judicial review*. During this process, the court declares legislation or presidential ordinance null in the case of "*ultra vires*", i.e., beyond one's legal authority or against the constitution's provisions. Interestingly, the concept of judicial review is not mentioned in the U.S. Constitution but is itself a result of judicial construction. It was introduced by the Supreme Court in its Marbury v. Madison (1803) case decision when it ruled that since the Constitution is the supreme law of the land, and the judiciary must uphold it, the courts have the right to declare unconstitutional any law of the states, the congress or even the executive if they are found to be inconsistent with the provisions of the Constitution.

Similarly, the federal structure of the United States, which the framers introduced, adds to the "exceptionalism" of the country. The United States was among the first countries to introduce a concept of *dual government* at the federal and state level to provide states a sense of autonomy to individual states. Similarly, various powers are further devolved to counties, districts, and other local units to allow multiple access points for citizens. Despite having a large geographical territory comprising 50 states and other political units, the United States' federal structure is arguably the most crucial factor behind its political stability and unity for over 230 years.

On the other hand, analysts often correlate the United States' exceptionalism with its intent and ability to play a unique and decisive role on the world stage. However, it is essential to note that it had a predominantly isolationist foreign policy doctrine before the 20th century. During Woodrow Wilson's presidency from 1913 to 1921, he initiated its internationalist (or what some call interventionist) approach to world affairs. During this time, America made a decisive entry into the First World War.

Chapter Seven

Democracy in the 20th Century – America proved its "exceptionalism"

The 20th century is generally characterized by the decay of colonialism, the rise of nationalism, the two world wars, nuclear power, and the cold war. However, a watershed moment was the overall restructuring of nations' political and social structures worldwide.

As America made a decisive entry into the world stage, it exhibited its great military strength and prowess and inspired other countries by displaying the essentiality of democracy over other forms of government. It did this by ensuring its citizens' prosperity and paved the way for meaningful consultations to attain sustainable international peace.

The First and Second world wars proved democracy to be triumphant

The First World War (WWI), colloquially known as "The Great War" by contemporaries, began in 1914 and ended in 1918. It was sparked by the assassination of Erzherzog Franz Ferdinand, the heir to the Austro-Hungarian Empire's throne, conducted in Sarajevo by Gavrilo Princip of the Bosnian Serb liberation movement "Young Bosnia." The war was fought primarily between two groups: the allies, or the "The Triple Entente" and the Axis, i.e., "The Central Powers". While the former included the British Empire, France, Italy, and Russia, the Axis included Germany, Austria-Hungary, Bulgaria, and the Ottoman Empire.

What served as the decisive turning point of the war was the entry of the United States into the World War against Germany in 1917. This entry happened following a vote of approval by the U.S. Senate. The war concluded with success for the allied powers, complemented by the 1919 Treaty of Versailles. This treaty was based on U.S. President Woodrow Wilson's 14th point, which resulted in the foundation of the League of Nations. America's entry under Wilson helped it become a world superpower and ushered in a new era of liberal internationalism. Democratic values were introduced to the world through international institutions, particularly the League of Nations, the first intergovernmental institution to provide a forum for resolving international disputes.

The end of the First World War proved to be a momentary success for democracy in Europe, as it was preserved in France and extended to Germany, albeit temporarily. However, in Finland, democratic norms had been established much earlier, when full modern democratic rights, universal suffrage for all citizens, a proportional representation, and an open list system were enshrined in the Constitution in 1906. Similarly, in Russia, the February Revolution in 1917 had led to a temporary period of liberal democracy under Alexander Kerensky until the October takeover by Lenin.

The Great Depression of the 1930s proved to be detrimental to the democratic forces around the world. While there was a rise in dictatorships in South America and Europe, it had the most detrimental effect on Germany. While the Treaty of Versailles had already punished Germany with severe war reparations, the Great Depression furthered the rise in unemployment and hyperinflation as U.S. banks called in all their foreign loans on short notice. While the democratic Weimar democracy had already been weakened due to the war, the preceding economic factors undermined Germans' faith in democracy. This led to the resignation of the German Chancellor, Hermann Muller, in March 1930. Hitler and his Nazi party capitalized on the political vacuum and the rise in nationalistic fervor and rose to power as the Chancellor of Germany.

Although the Second World War proved to be one of the deadliest wars in the history of humankind, it forced the world leaders, particularly from the Allied Countries, to discuss possibilities to forge a lasting peace. The negotiations resulted in the establishment of some of the key international organizations to establish peace and promote internationalism: these included theUnited Nations, World Bank, IMF, and NATO, amongst others.

The foundation of the United Nations

The United Nations Charter was discussed and prepared during the San Francisco Conference and signed on June 26, 1945, by 50 out of the 51 original member states. It came into force on

October 24, 1945, following approval by the five permanent member states of the UNSC - China, the Soviet Union, France, the United States, and the United Kingdom. The charter was later ratified by 193 countries, making it one of the most prominent international agreements. The charter requires the UN and its members to attain global peace and security, have mutual respect for the international law, achieve "better living standards" for their citizens and fight social, economic, and health inequalities. It also calls to promote "universal respect for, and observance of, human rights and fundamental freedoms for all without distinction of race, sex, language, or religion." Being the first document of international law and human rights, the acceptance of the UN charter across the world means a global consensus on democracy, a core value of the United Nations.

Wilson's 14 Points

While the United States had been a hesitant belligerent in the First World War, President Wilson's regime made several efforts to remain neutral. Near the end of the war, Woodrow Wilson enunciated his Fourteen Points, which he saw as the only pathway to true world peace. While these points served as a platform for future negotiations amongst the belligerents, it would be just to suggest that most contemporary-era democratic principles stem from them. Wilson had the following suggestions (or fourteen points), which he proclaimed in a famous speech to the Congress on January 8, 1918:

I. Open covenants of peace, openly arrived at, after which there shall be no private international understandings of any kind but diplomacy shall proceed always frankly and in the public view.

II. Absolute freedom of navigation upon the seas, outside territorial waters, alike in peace and in war, except as the seas may be closed in whole or in part by international action for the enforcement of international covenants.

III. The removal, so far as possible, of all economic barriers and the establishment of an equality of trade conditions among all the nations consenting to the peace and associating themselves for its maintenance.

IV. Adequate guarantees given and taken that national armaments will be reduced to the lowest point consistent with domestic safety.

V. A free, open-minded, and absolutely impartial adjustment of all colonial claims, based upon a strict observance of the principle that in determining all such questions of sovereignty the interests of the populations concerned must have equal weight with the equitable claims of the government whose title is to be determined.

VI. The evacuation of all Russian territory and such a settlement of all questions affecting Russia as will secure the best and freest cooperation of the other nations of the world in obtaining for her an unhampered and unembarrassed opportunity for the independent determination of her own political development and national policy and assure her of a sincere welcome into the society of free nations under institutions of her own choosing; and, more than a welcome, assistance also of every kind that she may need and may herself desire. The treatment accorded Russia by her sister nations in the months to come will be the acid test of their good will, of their comprehension of her needs as distinguished from their own interests, and of their intelligent and unselfish sympathy.

VII. Belgium, the whole world will agree, must be evacuated and restored, without any attempt to limit the sovereignty which she enjoys in common with all other free nations. No other single act will serve as this will serve to restore confidence among the nations in the laws which they have themselves set and determined for the government of their relations with one another. Without this healing act, the whole structure and validity of international law is forever impaired.

VIII. All French territory should be freed and the invaded portions restored, and the wrong done to France by Prussia in 1871 in the matter of Alsace-Lorraine, which has unsettled the peace of the world for nearly fifty years, should be righted, in order that peace may once more be made secure in the interest of all.

IX. A readjustment of the frontiers of Italy should be effected along clearly recognizable lines of nationality.

X. The peoples of Austria-Hungary, whose place among the nations we wish to see safeguarded and assured, should be accorded the freest opportunity of autonomous development.

XI. Rumania, Serbia, and Montenegro should be evacuated; occupied territories restored; Serbia accorded free and secure access to the sea; and the relations of the several Balkan states to one another determined by friendly counsel along historically established lines of allegiance and nationality; and international guarantees of the political and economic independence and territorial integrity of the several Balkan states should be entered into.

XII. The Turkish portions of the present Ottoman Empire should be assured a secure sovereignty, but the other nationalities which are now under Turkish rule should be assured an undoubted security of life and an absolutely unmolested opportunity of an autonomous development, and the Dardanelles should be permanently opened as a free passage to the ships and commerce of all nations under international guarantees.

XIII. An independent Polish state should be erected, which should include the territories inhabited by indisputably Polish populations, which should be assured a free and secure access to the sea, and whose political and economic independence and territorial integrity should be guaranteed by international covenant.

XIV. A general association of nations must be formed under specific covenants for the purpose of affording mutual guarantees of political independence and territorial integrity to great and small states alike.

Wilson's fourteen points held significant importance in several ways. Firstly, they portrayed various aspects of the ongoing American domestic policy reform (known as *progressivism*) in foreign policy. These included variants of domestic policy reforms, such as the principles of free trade, liberal agreements, and democracy. What made the fourteen points stand out as a foreign policy agenda was its sharp contrast to the prevalent notion of states that only self-interest should drive a state's foreign policy. Instead, Wilson argued that mutual trust and ethics should serve as the center of the foreign policy of a democratic state. Moreover, his notion of self-determination and the territorial integrity of states served as a prime motivator of decolonization and the independence of newly independent nation-states worldwide.

The Rise of America on the World Stage

The first World War proved to be a significant turning point for the United States as it heralded its significant position as a global military power. While America, in general, had been isolated from world affairs due to an inward-looking policy, Wilson's foreign policy and his fourteen points marked the beginning of its internationalist diplomatic era. This change was partly due to the rapid expansion of its military and technology industry, which supplied it with the means of diplomacy and boosted its economic status. Unfortunately, however, this was soon followed by a period of great repression that paved the way for the second World War and a series of religious, cultural, and social conflicts worldwide.

Following World War II, many Americans had questioned Wilson's internationalist approach and called for peace through *isolationism* and non-interventionism. America's relations with Latin American countries improved significantly under President Herbert Hoover, who was an anti-imperialist and introduced his "Good Neighbor Policy", renouncing America's right to intervene in Latin America under the Monroe Doctrine. The preceding non-interventionist policy was continued under the Roosevelt tenure, who ordered the removal of American troops from the Caribbean, adding vastly to America's overall prestige.

The Second World War again proved to be a decisive event where America proved its prowess and emerged as a world power. Following his re-election in 1940, Roosevelt sought to assist the Allies, including the Soviet Union, through his Lend-Lease Act. In August 1941, he met with the British Prime Minister Winston Churchill to discuss and issue a set of war objectives referred to as the Atlantic Charter. The Charter closely resembled Wilson's Fourteen Points as it called for national self-determination, free trade, maritime freedom, and disarmament, amongst others. Although there was significant domestic opposition to America's involvement in another war, Roosevelt continued with cautious optimism. However, the Japanese attack on Pearl Harbor proved to be a turning point, which amounted to the destruction of over 18 American ships and the loss of 2403 lives. Congress declared war on Japan on December 8, 1941, with only one dissenting vote. Three days later, Germany and Italy declared war on the United States, prompting a unanimous response from Congress. As a result of the attack on Pearl Harbor, the once-divided United States entered the global conflict with near-unanimity.

The United States' participation in World War II had ended isolation, and President Roosevelt was committed to preventing a return to isolationism once the war had ended. In December 1941, following a series of meetings, Roosevelt and Prime Minister Churchill announced the establishment of the United Nations, a wartime alliance of 26 countries. Roosevelt started planning for a postwar United Nations in 1943, meeting with congressional leaders to ensure congressional approval. The American public backed Roosevelt's efforts. Congress passed Fulbright and Connally resolutions (1943) that approved the United States' membership in an international body "with sufficient power to establish and maintain a just and lasting peace."

Although no war is truly "just", keeping in mind the horrors of Hiroshima and Nagasaki, the United States' involvement in World War II did have a silver lining. Roosevelt's post-war efforts had the resultant creation of peace-making institutions such as the United Nations, bringing a ray of hope for the world at large. Although the achievements of the United Nations vis-a-vis international disputes such as Palestine and Kashmir are subject to debate, one can not easily ignore its numerous contributions toward the maintenance of international peace and close cooperation amongst nation-states. In its absence, most countries lacked a forum for dialogue and consensus and preferred secret bilateral treaties over international ones. The

United Nations has provided a democratic forum for debate on crucial issues for all member states while assisting in drafting and executing various international treaties. While the UN has helped in the signage of over 560 multilateral treaties, here are some of the most prominent ones:

- 1948 Universal Declaration of Human Rights
- 1966 Racial Discrimination Convention
- 1966 Economic, Social and Cultural Rights Covenant
- 1987 Montreal Protocol
- 1992 UN Framework Convention on Climate Change
- 1992 Chemical Weapons Convention

Domestic Democratic Reforms in America

While America proved itself as a significant power on the world stage in the aftermath of the two world wars, it also underwent significant domestic reforms at the same time. These reforms ranged from socio-economic ones such as the Federal Reserve Act (1913) to guaranteeing women suffrage in 1920. These developments helped strengthen America's political system and paved the way for its progress and emergence as a legitimate torchbearer of democracy for the free world.

Feminist Waves

The campaign for women's suffrage began primarily in the decades leading up to the Civil War. During the 1820s and 1830s, most states extended the franchise to all white men, regardless of wealth or property. Also known as the first wave of feminism, the Suffragist movement sought to question the patriarchal foundations of this legislation, demanding a woman's equal right to vote. Besides vote, the movement was also concerned about the plights of single white middle-class women regarding their education, marriage, and employment. While targeting the preconceived notion that men and women had separate biologically determined roles in society, the activists sought to improve the legal position of women in various realms, particularly voting. The movement proved successful - first in New Zealand in 1893 when female suffrage was guaranteed. Later in America, in 1920, the Nineteenth Amendment to the U.S. Constitution provided American women the right to vote.

While the first feminist wave had led to the guaranteeing of voting rights for women, the second wave began in the 1960s and 1970s when feminist leaders argued that the legal and political rights extended to American women had not entirely resolved the "women's question". Viewing deep-rooted patriarchal norms and biological misconceptions about women as the primary reason behind their deprivation, the second wave of feminism argued for a cultural construction of gender. The movement bore fruits, as abortion was announced as legal through the famous 1973 case of Roe v. Wade - the first abortion case taken to the Supreme Court. Moreover, every state was required by law to have at least one abortion facility. The movement also resulted in the attainment of equal education and political rights for women, in continuation of the first wave. A milestone legislation passed in 1972, Titled IX, was a federal civil rights law prohibiting gender-based discrimination at any educational institution that receives financial assistance from the federal government.

Civil Rights Movement

The twentieth century also proved to be a turning point for anti-racial discrimination movements in America rooted in the eighteenth and nineteenth centuries. The Civil Rights movement reached its zenith during the 1950s and 1960s and sought social justice, particularly equal rights for Black Americans under American law. Although the Civil War had resulted in the official abolishment of slavery, it had not wholly ended racism and anti-racial prejudices against the black community. Many African Americans had to endure discrimination and violence, particularly in the southern states. As a result, they mobilized along with several White Americans to fight for their equality. They particularly targeted the "Jim Crow" laws prevalent in the South and restricted access to Black Americans for various public facilities such as education and transport. Moreover, while interracial marriage had been declared illegal, they were also denied the right to vote. While such segregation was not prevalent in the northern states, such racial segregation had gained legitimacy following the infamous Plessey vs. Ferguson case, where the Supreme Court declared that public facilities for Whites and Black Americans could be "separate but equal".

The Civil Rights movement particularly gained ground during World War II. Although the American war economy was booming, Black Americans were often denied the same socio-economic opportunities as their white counterparts. As several thousand Black Americans announced to march to the Capitol to demand their equal rights, President Roosevelt issued Executive Order 8802, which was aimed at opening military and other public jobs to all Americans, regardless of their racial, sexual, or national background.

During the Cold War, President Truman followed a Civil Rights Agenda, which was meant to end discrimination in the military and initiate grass-roots initiatives to implement anti-segregation laws and diminish racialism. An important turning point was the Rosa Parks incident when in 1955, a 55-year-old Black woman Rosa Parks declined the bus driver's request to vacate her seat for a

White passenger. Upon refusal, Rosa Parka was arrested, which infuriated the Black community who staged a 381-day boycott against the Montgomery Bus System, encouraging the Supreme Court on November 14, 1956, to declare segregated seating as illegal.

Similar instances and prolonged campaigns by the American community at large encouraged the promulgation of the Civil Rights Act of 1957 by President Eisenhower. This act was the first major Civil Rights Law since the Reconstruction Era. The legislation allowed federal officials to prosecute any individual found to have prevented anyone from voting. Furthermore, it also established a federal commission to investigate any allegations of voter fraud.

The twentieth century was a turning point for democracy throughout the world. While the two world wars resulted in enormous bloodshed and financial losses, they may have provided the aggressors with an opportunity to introspect and establish newer, sustainable models of world peace. The establishment of the United Nations and international economic agencies such as the World Bank and IMF can be seen as steps in the right direction. They have not only provided member-states worldwide the ability to progress through mutual agreements but also deepened the spirit of democracy internationally, particularly in once authoritarian states such as Turkey and Japan. Most importantly, Wilson and Roosevelt's idea of open negotiations based on morality and ethics instead of secret bilateral treaties among states has assisted the aspirations for sustainable world peace.

Moreover, democracy as a whole can be said to have strengthened domestically in America during the previous century. Whenever one speaks of democracy, one can not ignore the strong values of equality and inclusiveness. Although the American political system was meant to revolve around the preceding since its advent, women and racial minorities felt alienated from the political system in numerous regards. For example, while blacks had the right to vote by the end of the 19th century, they were victims of racial prejudice, and while women had the right to inheritance, they did not have the right to vote. The twentieth-century developments in America addressed these inequalities, as women were finally granted the right to vote, while legislation such as the Civil Rights Act of 1957 addressed racial disparities at a grass-root level.

However, despite these positive developments, it is regrettable that true world peace still seems to be a utopic ideal, keeping in mind the conflicts between nations such as the United States and Iran, the United States and China, India and Pakistan, and Israel and Palestine. While one may question the United Nations' ability to resolve these conflicts, the onus also falls on the individual states themselves for not establishing sustainable peace through negotiation.

During the twentieth century, America's democratic system flourished, and the country proved itself as a great power on the world stage. However, its credibility as a world power and a democracy has generally decreased in recent years. This decrease can be attributed to several factors, ranging from its increased intervention and subsequent military and political failures in the Middle East, particularly Iraq and Afghanistan, to a rapid rise in right-wing populism and anti-immigrant hatred since 2016.

Chapter Eight

Comparative Democracies

While the United States has been subject to most criticism regarding its eroding democratic ethos in recent years, evidence suggests that besides a few exceptions, democracy in most countries worldwide has generally taken a backseat. This change raises an important question: which countries are more democratic, and why?

The Economist Group, a UK-based private company that publishes the weekly newspaper The Economist, has a research division called The Economist Intelligence Unit (EIU). EIU is responsible for compiling something called a Democracy Index. While the index is generally similar to the Human Development Index, it primarily focuses on political institutions and freedoms and claims to evaluate the condition of democracy across 167 countries and territories, 166 of which are sovereign nations and 164 of which are UN member states. The index is based on 60 indicators divided into five categories that assess electoral process and pluralism, civil liberties, political culture, and political participation. In addition to a numerical score and a ranking, the index divides countries into four regime types: full democracies, flawed democracies, *hybrid regimes*, and authoritarian regimes.

Here is an overview of the recent 2020 Democracy Index for the different types of Regimes:

Full Democracies

Score: 8.01 - 10
Countries: 23
World Population percentage: 8.4%
GDP Percentage: 27.5%

Flawed Democracies

Score: 6.01 - 8
Countries: 52
World Population percentage: 41%
GDP Percentage: 45.7%

Hybrid regimes

Score: 4.01 - 6
Countries: 35
World Population percentage: 15%
GDP Percentage: 3.7%

Authoritarian regimes

Score: 0 - 4
Countries: 57
World Population percentage: 35.6%
GDP Percentage: 23.1%

Among the full democracies, the most prominent ones were Norway (1), Iceland (2), and Canada (5), while the United States was characterized as a flawed democracy. On the other hand, the authoritarian regimes included China, Russia, and Cuba, amongst others. The sharp differences in these statistics give rise to an important question: why are some countries fully democratic while others are entirely authoritarian?

To explain these differences, we need to analyze these countries on a case-to-case basis.

The Nordic Countries

The term "Nordic Countries" is generally used for Iceland, Norway, Sweden, Finland, and Denmark. Since all of these countries were ranked in the top ten on the democracy index (Norway 1, Iceland 2, Sweden 3, Finland 6, Denmark 7), one is prompted to delve into the reasons behind their success. The sociopolitical and economic framework within which the Nordic roughly operate is usually referred to as the "Nordic Model". While it was developed in the 1930s under the rule of social democrats, the Nordic Model became famous mostly following the second World War.

With regards to their political system, the three Scandinavian countries (Norway, Sweden, and Denmark) are constitutional monarchies, while Finland and Iceland are republics. According to the recent democracy index, all Nordic Countries have been described as being highly democratic, having a *unicameral* legislature, and using proportional representation in their elections. While there are differences among the Nordic countries, they have a range of commonalities. Among these is a consensus on the need for a universalist welfare state to increase individual autonomy and enhance social mobility. Moreover, these countries support a *corporatist* economic system where labor representatives and employers negotiate wage rates while the government mediates the labor market policy. The Nordic countries are also committed to private ownership within a mixed economy, except for Norway, where the state owns a large number of enterprises.

Besides the Democracy Index, the Nordic countries have also ranked highly on other statistics such as the Human Development Index (HDI), the Global Peace Index, and the World Happiness Report. The Nordic model has altered in certain aspects in recent decades, such as the increased deregulation and privatization of public services. However, it still stands out amongst other models, emphasizing social welfare and public services.

The model primarily emerged from a mixture of social democratic, *centrist*, and right-wing political parties, particularly in Finland and Iceland, alongside the welfare approach that resulted from the "great compromise" between capital and labor. The overall state's expenditure on social security was reduced in the 1980s and 1990s following the financial crises. However, the general welfare expenditure in these countries remained high compared to their other European counterparts.

The United States

The United States was downgraded from a full democracy to a flawed democracy in 2016. Its score dropped from 8.05 in 2015 to 7.98 following the election of Donald Trump in 2016. The analysis, however, noted that this was caused not simply by Trump's victory but by several factors dating back to at least the late 1960s that have damaged Americans' faith in governmental institutions. Although many saw Biden's win in 2020 as a positive milestone for democracy, as the United States saw increasing political involvement with record voter turnout and campaigns to confront racial inequality, the country's score yet fell to 7.92 for the year. The EIU report explained this as "popular faith in the democratic process was given a hit by Donald Trump and many of his followers' reluctance to accept the election outcome" (Swann et al., 2021).

Most analysts argue that the American democracy is eroding due to a plethora of factors, the most significant one being institutional flaws, particularly regarding the electoral college. Experts argue that although democracy is founded on majority rule and the notion that every individual's vote counts, five American presidents during the last twenty years have been elected despite losing the popular vote. The most prominent examples include George W. Bush in 2000, who lost the popular vote by 500,000 votes, and Donald Trump in 2016 by about 3 million votes. This is because under the American Electoral College system, a group of elected representatives in each state vote for the president using a winner-takes-all model. The framers of the Constitution initially designed the system to count slave populations in the less-populated southern states and not to overburden either the public or the congress in selecting the president. However, the recent electoral results have deepened the urban-rural divide and resulted in a select-few states attaining disproportionate power and dominance.

Besides the electoral process, analysts also argue that the American democracy faces several institutional weaknesses, such as gerrymandering. This practice is still widely used by political parties to manipulate the boundaries of a particular electoral constituency to favor their electoral outcomes. Similarly, as discussed in our earlier chapter, filibustering is still used by members of Congress to obstruct legislation on some of the essential subjects, including taxation and foreign policy. Most recently, the attack on the Capitol on January 6, 2021, was an event unprecedented in the history of American democracy. As the joint session of the congress was meeting to count electoral votes and ratify the election of Joe Biden, a mob of 2,000 to 2500 supporters of Donald Trump attacked the Capitol Building to overturn his defeat in the 2020 elections.

Keeping in mind the fragility of the American democracy, various analysts have prescribed ways to fix and strengthen it. For example, a former congressman Tom Coleman made three proposals to improve democracy, each possible through congressional action. Amongst these proposals, the most prominent one is the need to establish a new court meant to resolve the disputes between the president and congress. This new court becomes necessary, particularly in light of the Trump era when the administration was directed not to cooperate with the impeachment investigation -an effective delay tactic. According to Coleman, this court becomes necessary, particularly in the cases of impeachment proceedings that must not face unnecessary delays.

Moreover, he suggests that, unfortunately, many Americans have been unable to differentiate between acceptable and unacceptable political traits, such as autocratic tendencies in the case of Trump. Often, the president's inappropriate behavior (including near-criminal behavior) has been ignored by many. One reason is the avalanche of information supplied due to unregulated social media. This behavior highlights the lack of teaching of U.S. civic education in educational institutions. While it is vital for the government to tackle disinformation through various channels such as print, electronic and social media, it must also assist the development of educational programs that teach citizens civic values and the principles of democracy. Besides the preceding, reforms are also required regarding the electoral college, the voting procedures, and gerrymandering, amongst others.

The Case of Taiwan

According to the 2020 Democracy Index, Taiwan was the only country whose democracy score increased by over one point. It reached 8.94 from 7.73 in 2019, leaving behind Japan and South Korea to become the highest-ranked democracy in Asia. What factored this rise was a successful election in 2019 alongside a series of legal and legislative reforms in recent years. According to the Economist Intelligence Unit, Taiwan "demonstrated the resilience of its democracy when electoral processes, parliamentary oversight, and civil liberties have been backsliding globally" (Li, 2021).

The overall public confidence in their government also increased following its reasonable handling of the Covid-19 pandemic. Several analysts described this success as better than other countries, including South Korea and Japan. The increased public support following Taiwanese President Tsai Ing-wen's clash with Chinese President Xi Jinping is another important reason. She told him the island would not accept a "one country, two systems" arrangement with China.

To understand the evolution of democracy in Taiwan and its sharp contrast with the authoritarian model of the People's Republic of China, one needs to delve into the recent histories of both countries. In 1945, following the conclusion of World War II, the nationalist government of the Republic of China (ROC) was led by the Kuomintang (KMT), which took control of Taiwan, however, without a formal transfer of territorial sovereignty. During the Chinese Civil War (1927-1949), the KMT, mainly under the leadership of Chiang Kai-shek, fought against the Chinese Communist Party (CCP) forces and subsequently lost control of mainland China, thus withdrawing to Taiwan where Chiang Kai-shek declared martial law. CCP established the People's Republic of China on the mainland while the ROC government retreated to the island of Taiwan. Nevertheless, the Kuomintang continued to rule Taiwan as a single-party state for forty years until the 1980s, when the democratic reforms were introduced, paving the way for the first presidential election in 1996. After the war, Taiwan underwent rapid economic growth, referred to as the "Taiwan Miracle", and became known as one of the "Four Asian Tigers".

The initial economic reforms were driven primarily by the immediate aftermath of World War II and the Chinese Civil War. These had caused severe inflation, while a flawed monetary policy and corruption had further exacerbated the situation. This situation was tackled successfully by the KMT authorities with a range of economic reforms. These reforms included a land reform program, *liberalization*, and industrialization.

On the political front, until the 1970s, the Republic of China (the former Chinese government that escaped to Taiwan) was acknowledged as the only legal government of China by the United Nations and most western states. At the same time, the People's Republic of China (the newly formed Chinese government established by the Chinese Communist Party) was not recognized, primarily due to the Cold War. Moreover, until the late 1980s, the KMT administered Taiwan under martial law, with the declared objective of being cautious against Communist infiltration and preparing to reclaim mainland China (Project National Glory). As such, political opposition was not tolerated.

However, by the late 1970s and 1980s, several Taiwanese who had initially felt left behind by the economic reforms became part of the country's new middle class. As a result of the free market economy and industrialization, the Taiwanese now had a vital bargaining chip in their calls for political reform. What served as a turning point for politics in Taiwan was the Kaohsiung

Incident (or the Formosa Incident), as it led to a successful movement for democratization in Taiwan. The incident stemmed in 1978 when following America's tacit acknowledgment of the PRC's One-China principle, U.S. President Carter announced to sever official ties with the Republic of China on January 1, 1979. President Chiang Ching-Kuo promptly postponed all elections without specifying a timetable for their resumption. Tangwai, an opposition party with rapidly growing popularity, was deeply angered and dismayed by Chiang's decision since it halted the solely authorized mechanism of expressing their thoughts.

Infuriated Tangwai leader Huang Hsin-Chieh and his allies soon appealed to the KMT government to restore the elections, but their request was turned down. On January 21, 1979, the KMT arrested Yu Teng-fa, another tangwai leader, falsely accusing him of supporting the Chinese Communist Party. This action was viewed by the Tangwai as a sign of total repression, which made them decide to conduct street protests against the government. These actions resulted in an intensifying clash between the KMT and the Tangwai.

In May 1979, the Tangwai leader Huang Hsin-Chieh introduced the Formosa Magazine, which aimed to increase the party's membership. The magazine applied for a permit to conduct a human rights forum on December 10, 1979, at an indoor stadium, but the request was denied. As a result, the party decided to conduct the event at the Kaohsiung Headquarters instead. However, when two campaign wagons were sent to broadcast the "Human Rights Forum", the vehicles were seized by the police. When the event was conducted on the evening of December 10, the police deliberately marched forward and closed in on the demonstrators with the intent of creating panic and chaos. This action was repeated and resulted in a clash of the demonstrators with the forces sent by KMT. The KMT regime arrested many opposition leaders using this incident as an excuse, imprisoning some for over two months.

The KMT government further lost legitimacy on the international stage as the United Nations passed the resolution 2758 which "the representatives of Chiang Kai-shek (or the Republic of China) were removed from the UN and replaced by the People's Republic of China". Following Chiang Kai-shek's death in 1975, his successor Yen Chia-kan chose to gradually loosen political controls and transition towards democracy, allowing opposition parties to conduct meetings or publish magazines. His successor Lee Teng-Hui continued to democratize the government, transferring more government authority to local Taiwanese citizens and following a policy of "Taiwanization", promoting local culture and history over a pan-China perspective.

The Kuomintang's (KMT) dominance ended in the 2000 presidential elections. Chen Shui-bian, the Democratic Progressive Party (DPP) candidate, defeated independent James Soong (previously of the Kuomintang) and Kuomintang candidate Lien Chan in a three-way contest and was elected with 39% of the vote. In addition, between 2002 and 2007, the government under Chen Sui-Bian conducted a series of Taiwanization reforms which included replacing terms such as "China", "Taipei", and others that indicated the relevance of Chinese culture with "Taiwan" on official documents, including the passports. Chen Sui Bian further adopted a Westernized writing style for official documents and changed the official year from the Chinese year to the Gregorian year, terming it a "concentrated effort to globalize Taiwan's ossified bureaucracy and upgrade the nation's competitive advantage".

In the 2008 elections, however, the KMT regained control of the legislature as its candidate Ma Ying-jeou promised friendlier relations with China and economic reforms. The KMT was reelected in 2012 but failed to satisfy the public as students conducted a widespread rally and occupied the parliament building in April 2014, terming it an outrage against the "undemocratic methods used by the KMT". Although the KMT government promised to delay the ratification of an agreement with China initiated without a proper debate, this event had far-reaching consequences as it shifted the public's tilt towards the DPP. In the 2016 elections, the DPP secured 56% of the vote, becoming the first non-KMT party to win an outright majority in the parliament. DPP's anti-China rhetoric and promises for greater democratic reforms allowed them to be reelected again during the January 2020 presidential election.

The preceding analysis illustrates how democracy has evolved in Taiwan ever since the Kuomintang took control of the island following their defeat to the Communist Party in 1949. The ROC continued to have an authoritarian regime under the leadership of Chiang Kai-Shek. However, the increasing calls for democratization have led his successors to loosen political control and increase political liberalization. While the People's Republic of China continues to be dominated by a single party (the Chinese Communist Party) ever since its inception, Taiwan has seen several non-KMT governments coming into power through electoral *mandates* - such as the DPP.

The Gulf States

The Arab states of the Persian Gulf (commonly referred to as GCC countries) include Saudi Arabia, Kuwait, Bahrain, Qatar, the UAE, and Oman. All Arab Gulf States have traditionally received a score of under 3.0 points on the Democracy Index, serving as the most relevant examples of authoritarian states. While Saudi Arabia has historically remained the most authoritarian state, receiving a score of 2.08, Qatar fares better at 3.24 points. This difference may be explained by the fact that Saudi Arabia and Oman are absolute monarchies, with the monarch ruling on their own. On the other hand, others, such as Qatar and Bahrain, are semi-constitutional democracies with separate heads of government. However, the royalty still wields enormous legislative or executive powers.

In Saudi Arabia, the king holds legislative, executive, and judicial powers and uses royal decrees as the basis of legislation. The king is also the prime minister and chairs the council of ministers, typically members of the Al-Saud (royal family). While the totalitarian nature of the state is rooted in its Islamic and tribal history, the state's political system has been accused of being the reason behind the lack of civil liberties such as religious freedom and intolerance for political dissent in the country. Moreover, the ruling family has often been accused of systemic corruption and bribery. In 2010, Transparency International assigned Saudi Arabia a score of 4.7 in its Corruption Perceptions Index (on a scale from 0 to 10 where 0 is "highly corrupt" and 10 is "highly clean"). Although the regime has initiated several political and social reforms, such as improving public transparency, efficiency, and good governance, nepotism and *cronyism* remain prevalent. While anti-corruption laws are selectively enforced, government officials openly engage in corruption. The government also quashes dissent with force. In November 2017, several senior Saudi Arabian princes and higher officials, including Prince Al-Waleed bin Talal, were detained in Saudi Arabia. Similarly, the Saudi government has been accused of killing the Saudi journalist Jamal Khashoggi for showing his dissent against the regime's policies.

However, on the other hand, it is worth mentioning that the country's ranking has improved by 0.15 points for 2020. This improvement can be attributed to several socio-economic liberalization policies by the country's de facto ruler, Crown Prince Muhammad bin Salman. While several Saudis have tacitly opposed Muhammad's domestic reform agenda, his policies are primarily aimed at rebranding the country's image internationally. As such, his policies include reducing the powers of the religious police, allowing female citizens to drive, and weakening the male-guardianship system in 2019. Moreover, Muhammad bin Salman has also announced plans to introduce several other legal reforms to modernize the country to attract more tourism and foreign investors.

In a similar vein, the state of Qatar has also recently taken steps to improve its international image by undertaking a series of modernization reforms, particularly as it hosts the FIFA World Cup in 2022. While some critics have described it as a "PR stunt", almost fifty years after its establishment, the country announced that it would hold its first general election of a consultative assembly (the Shura) in October 2021. Before these elections, the locals could only vote in local elections or referendums on the constitution. According to Ahmed Yousef al-Mlifi, a political analyst in Kuwait, "The election of the Shura Council represents a new experience. Even if the result is not a truly democratic parliament, but rather an advisory body, it is still a step toward democracy (Deutsche Welle, 2021) ."

One may realize that despite gradual moves towards political and economic liberalization in the Gulf States, the calls for democracy are not as discernible as those in the non-Gulf Arab states, as evidenced during the Arab Spring. Majorities in the Gulf States are generally satisfied with the social security systems in their countries, such as education, healthcare, and other sources of subjective wellbeing. What political sociologists may describe as "performance legitimacy", the regimes in these rentier states possess great wealth given their oil and energy resources, which they can adequately spend on the wellbeing of their citizens and expatriates. As a result, these states have maintained a political order based on clientelism and patronage. As long as citizens are guaranteed sufficient wealth and social security, the regimes, albeit authoritarian, can retain their legitimacy.

China

The People's Republic of China is widely known as one of the most authoritarian countries in the world. In the recent Democracy Index of 2020, China was ranked 151st with a score of 2.27. As previously mentioned, the Communist Party of China took control of mainland China following its success in the Civil War in 1949 against the Kuomintang (KMT) and has ever since retained control over the country. Under an authoritarian, one-party system of government, the Chinese Communist Party exercises vast executive, legislative and judicial powers. The CCP is headed by the General Secretary, who serves as China's Paramount Leader. The state power is exercised by the CCP primarily through the National People's Congress (NPC), the president, and the Central People's Government (State Council), along with its regional and local representative bodies. On the other hand, Hong Kong and Macau, China's two unique administrative regions (SARs), have independent multi-party systems distinct from the mainland's one-party system.

Given the authoritarian nature of the political system, there are publicly elected national leaders, no tolerance for political dissent, and a lack of civil liberties such as freedom of speech and religious freedom, amongst others. In addition, the Chinese Communist Party directly controls and leads the People's Liberation Army, which was initially the party's militia but became the state's army following the PRC's establishment in 1949. As such, the military is an important institution used by the Communist Party to maintain its legitimacy amongst the public.

While China is amongst the least democratic states, its recent rise as an economic giant has given rise to whether democracy is a prerequisite for economic growth. Most contemporary economists argue that authoritarian regimes provide fewer prospects for economic growth and cultural improvement than democratic ones. Scholars such as Milton Friedman (1962) argued that higher legal protections facilitated economic development. Further, many other studies suggest that democracy promotes economic liberalization and that democracy is favorable for long-term and sustainable economic growth (Fidrmuc, 2001; Peev & Mueller, 2012). However, the economic rise of China has proved to be a significant challenge to these hypotheses.

Analysts argue that with an increase in economic liberalization, the pace of economic growth improves as well. While China envisions a "Chinese style *Socialism*" intending to increase economic growth, the Chinese government has at the same time initiated various economic liberalization reforms. For example, while the Chinese Communist Party denies using free-market mechanisms, many financial analysts believe China has opened its markets. As such, its economic progress is inextricably linked to politics. The Chinese government tends to promote economic growth using its unlimited authority to intervene in certain economic transactions while seeking to liberalize the economy.

Regarding the legal system, critics argue that the law is subject to the leaders rather than the other way around in China's authoritarian system. China's leaders practice rule by law rather than conforming to the law as is more usual in constitutional democracies. Although after Mao's death, legal changes took place, and a formal judicial system was established, it remains subordinate to the party leadership, which frequently shields officials from the law. International human-rights activists have also criticized China for its desire to use the death penalty and "rehabilitation" centers, particularly for the minorities such as the Uyghur community.

As a whole, China has undergone significant economic growth in the recent decades, with its growth rate not falling below 7.5 ever since the Asian financial crisis and its GDP per capita increasing rapidly. However, its citizens still lack adequate access to a range of fundamental rights guaranteed in most Western democracies. While the PRC mandates and implements censorship on electronic, print, and social media, the minorities such as the Uyghurs have to undergo arbitrary detentions and punishments. Similarly, critics of the Chinese government are dealt with with an iron fist. During the 709 crackdown, which began in 2015, more than 200 attorneys, legal assistants, and dissidents, including Jiang Tianyong, were arrested and/or incarcerated. Authorities in the People's Republic of China claim to define human rights differently, including economic, social, and political rights, all connected to the country's "national culture" and degree of development. Using this criterion, authorities in the People's Republic of China assert that human rights are improving. However, they do not follow the definition adopted by most nations and organizations. PRC leaders have consistently said that the "Four Cardinal Principles" transcend citizenship rights under the PRC Constitution. These principles have a cultural interpretation and include propriety, righteousness, integrity, and shame. Officials in the PRC view the supremacy of the Four Cardinal Principles as a legal foundation for arresting people who, according to the government, tend to subvert the principles.

The United Kingdom

The United Kingdom is considered one of the torchbearers of democracy, a fact well-represented by its high score of 8.54 on the 2020 democracy index, which gives it a rank of 16th in the list of most democratic countries. Moreover, as discussed in our previous chapters, the United Kingdom can be considered the cradle of modern democracy, provided the political developments in the country beginning from the introduction of the Magna Carta in 1215, the Bill of Rights in 1689, and the overall development of a robust parliamentary system of governance.

The United Kingdom is essentially a unitary state within the framework of a parliamentary democracy under a constitutional monarchy where the Crown is vested with ceremonial powers (i.e., the Queen being the Head of State). At the same time, the Prime Minister is the head of the government. The British Government (which is derived from the parliament) exercised executive authority on behalf and consent of the Crown. Executive power is also devolved to the governments of Scotland, Wales, and Northern Ireland. Legislative powers belong to the two houses of the UK parliament, i.e., the House of Lords and the House of Commons, as well as the Scottish and Welsh parliaments.

An interesting element about the case of UK's democracy is that its constitution is un-codified, unlike most other democracies such as the USA and France. Instead, it is a loose collection of constitutional conventions, legislations, and other elements. As a result, the system of government in the United Kingdom is commonly referred to as the Westminster system. It has been adopted by various countries worldwide, particularly those that were a part of the British Empire.

The Conservative Party and the Labour Party have been the two major parties since the 1920s. Prior to the rise of the Labour Party in British politics, the Liberal Party, together with the Conservatives, was the other main political party. While coalition and minority governments have occasionally been a feature of parliamentary politics, the first-past-the-post electoral system used for general elections tends to maintain these two parties' dominance. However, both parties have relied on a third party, such as the Liberal Democrats, to deliver a working majority in Parliament occasionally.

While the United Kingdom's democracy is idealized by countries around the globe, critics argue that democracy may be failing, particularly following Brexit.

As Kenneth Rogoff (2016) notes, *"The real lunacy of the United Kingdom's vote to leave the European Union was not that British leaders dared to ask their populace to weigh the benefits of membership against the immigration pressures it presents. Rather, it was the absurdly low bar for exit, requiring only a simple majority. Given voter turnout of 70 percent, this meant that the leave campaign won with only 36 percent of eligible voters backing it. This isn't democracy; it is Russian roulette for republics. A decision of enormous consequence — far greater even than amending a country's constitution (of course, the United Kingdom lacks a written one) — has been made without any appropriate checks and balances"*.

While the ability of the UK's majority to vote for a major foreign policy decision may be seen as democratic by many, others believe that a healthy democratic political system does not only entail a voice of the public but also voters' knowledge about the effects of their decision, as well as a range of checks and balances to ensure political stability. According to UK's ex-Prime Minister Gordon Brown, many Britons are dissatisfied with the way the country is governed by a select few elites in London. A Guardian report (2021) suggests that the recent polls conducted in Scotland indicated that 49% of voters wanted Scotland to be independent as opposed to 44% who opposed it. The Covid-19 pandemic has arguably exposed the differences amongst the devolved regions of the UK, as the Scottish and Welsh first ministers complained they were not consulted during the healthcare policy formation phase. Brown suggests that besides enhancing coordination, the government must improve its general outreach to the public, preferably by setting up citizens' assemblies across various regions of the country.

India

India's points on the Democracy Index have fallen sharply, from being nearly a full democracy with 7.92 points in 2014 to becoming a flawed democracy with 6.61 points in 2020. According to another report on democracy by the Sweden-based V-Dem Institution, India has been termed an "electoral *autocracy*" (Biswas, 2021).

Soon after its independence from colonial rule in 1947, India's political leaders had advocated for and distinguished the notions of *secularism* and diversity in the country's constitution. The need for such stemmed from the country's multi-ethnic and multi-religious demographic nature - while Hindus formed the majority, a significant proportion of about 20% of the population comprised Muslims, Sikhs, and Christians, among other minority religious groups. However, analysts argue that since 2014, India under Mr. Modi and his Hindu nationalist party, BJP's government has meant a backsliding of secularism and an ushering of religious and caste-based politics.

They claim that under Mr. Modi's rule, there has been increased pressure on human rights organizations, harassment of journalists and activists, and a wave of violence, particularly targeting the Muslim community. This change has resulted in a worsening of the country's political and civil rights.

Chapter Nine

Factors Behind the Erosion of Democracy

A ccording to Daniel Ziblatt, a renowned political scientist, "Beginning with the so-called "third wave" of democratization, and especially following the collapse of the Soviet Union, many observers and policymakers concluded that authoritarianism was on the decline and that democracy had become, as the expression was in the 1990s, "the only game in town." That era of self-confidence has passed." Ziblatt correctly quotes the cases of China, Russia, and most Middle Eastern states where authoritarianism has not diminished but instead gained ground. Moreover, several states worldwide have witnessed a sharp departure from democratic norms and values, with prominent examples including Thailand, India, and Venezuela. As Pakistani military general Pervez Musharraf ousted a democratically elected government in 1992, he faced little resistance to legitimizing his ten-year military rule as the civil society preferred "performance legitimacy" over "democratic injustice".

On the other hand, one may think of democracy to be in a recession as we think about the rise of populism and anti-immigrant rhetoric in vast parts of Europe and the United States, as evidenced by the election of Donald Trump. Populism is a significant threat to democracy in the contemporary era, as it has arguably led to polarisation and a rise in socio-economic inequalities. In the case of India, while populism has been prevalent in some forms ever since its independence from colonial rule in 1947, the election of the BJP, a Hindu populist party, has come to serve as an anti-thesis of the country's secular credentials. Rather than inclusion, equality, or social justice, analysts such as Prashant Jha (2017) have termed the contemporary political situation in India as akin to the subversion and the collapse of the Indian political system at large at the hands of a single political entity. Moreover, the recent years have seen a sharp rise in pro-majoritarian and anti-minority legislation such as the "Citizenship Amendment Bill" that deliberately denies the right of citizenship to Muslim immigrants and the annulment of Article 370, which provided a special autonomous status to the state of Kashmir.

Similarly, in the case of the United States, immediately following the 2016 presidential election, Donald Trump announced a series of anti-immigrant policies merely on ethnic or religious lines, which threatened the very liberal democratic ideals of the American democracy. Hence, the challenge of immigration and sustaining multi-ethnic democracies, such as the United States, is a significant concern for most political analysts.

Economic Inequality and Democratic Discontent

Performance legitimacy is a term often used by political theorists such as Y Zhu (2011) to refer to political support given to political regimes conditionally based on their performance - regardless of whether they are democratic or not. Whereas several nation-states such as Japan, Korea, and Canada have proven their democratic system to be the factor behind their rapid progress, the rise in inequalities in other states has generally sparked public discontent against democracy in vast parts of the world. The cases include those of various Latin American countries such as Venezuela, where the public has tended to support non-democratic regimes over democratic ones due to the latter's failure on the economic front.

Corruption and Inefficiency

Bribery, corruption, and *red-tapism* are prevalent in vast parts of the developing world and serve as a significant reason behind the general public's discontent with their political systems. Further, a recent Transparency International research analysis shows a negative correlation between corruption and the overall health of democracies, suggesting that countries with minimal corruption were likely to be more robust democracies and vice-versa. The top countries included New Zealand and Denmark, which most effectively minimized corruption and had the highest scores for democratic strength (87 and 88, respectively). On the other hand, countries that had failed to make serious inroads against corruption were most likely to score lower in terms of democratic strength, with Somalia, Syria, and South Sudan with the lowest scores of 10, 13, and 13, respectively.

Internal Structural Flaws

Most established democracies have constitutions and democratic institutions that were originally introduced over two to three centuries ago. Although these institutions and norms are a matter of pride for most citizens, others argue they are ill-suited for a range of contemporary challenges faced by these democracies, such as multi-ethnicity and immigration. For instance, while most Americans take pride in their constitution, others term institutions such as the Electoral College as dysfunctional. They target the electoral college to be an unjust institution as it provides unequal voting power to individuals based on where they live as smaller states tend to be favored with more electoral votes per person. For instance, every individual's vote in Wyoming counts over four times as much in the Electoral College as someone from Texas.

Similarly, while gerrymandering (i.e., manipulating electoral district boundaries to favor one party over the other) may have decreased, it is still prevalent. Political strategies in America still tend to use the two tactics: "cracking", i.e., diminishing the voting power of the opposition party's supporters across several districts, and "packing", i.e., concentrating an opposition party's voters in a single district to diminish their voting power in other districts.

Another major structural flaw is filibustering, which is still prevalent in the American congress and impedes several important legislation. It is a political practice in which one or more members of a congress or parliament discuss a proposed piece of legislation to postpone or completely prohibit a decision on the proposal from being taken. It is regarded as an obstruction in a legislative or other decision-making body, also referred to as "talking a bill to death" or "talking out a bill." Filibustering is frequently initiated by senators whose policy initiatives have failed and who are always ready to prepare and start their own filibusters. A famous example of this is the case of Senator Fillman (1905), who began reading from Childe Harold, a long poem by Lord Byron, declaring that he would continue to do so until the clauses he proposed were removed from the bill under consideration and he had proved successful.

Henceforth, one could suggest that wide-ranging factors hurdle democracy. While radicalization and majoritarian-led politics are some of the critical threats to democracy, corruption and economic inequalities only further exacerbate the problem. Moreover, in the case of the United States, various other internal factors such as the electoral college, gerrymandering, and filibustering serve as some of the significant challenges to democracy. However, what serves as a light at the end of the tunnel is the American democracy's resilience, as evident in the 2020 elections.

Chapter Ten

Cautious Optimism

"**A**fter just 100 days, I can report to the nation, America is on the move again: turning peril into possibility, crisis into opportunity, setbacks to strength", remarked U.S. President Joe Biden in his speech to the Congress upon completion of his 100 days in office. According to an ABC News poll conducted in May 2021, 64 percent of Americans showed optimism that the country was on the right track, including around four in ten Republicans (Moore, 2021). Biden's election as president came at a critical juncture in American history. While the overall confidence of Americans in their political system had declined sharply during the preceding four years of Donald Trump's presidency, the Covid-19 pandemic and the mishandling thereof only added to the exasperation of the laypeople.

The recent elections may be viewed as a positive development for American democracy due to several factors. First, regarding the domestic political scene during Trump's presidency, right-wing populism and anti-immigrant rhetoric had led to polarisation and fragmentation of the American society along political and ethnic lines. The recent election is being viewed by many as the return of a "democratic America" marked by liberal notions of equality, liberty, and freedom of speech. Several years ago, John

Stuart Mill pointed out that "tyranny of the majority" is one of the inherent weaknesses of majority rule. Here the majority of the electorate pursues objectives that are exclusive to them, often at the cost of the minorities. The United States feared a similar state of affairs due to increased anti-immigrant rhetoric and white supremacy. Biden's election campaign was based on racial equality and egalitarianism. As such, his success is being seen by many as a positive development. For instance, with regards to immigration, as opposed to Trump's generally anti-immigration rhetoric and policies such as the "Border Wall", Biden's government raised the refugee quota for the financial year 2021 from 15,000 to 62,500 to increase the United States' capacity to accept more refugees in the following years.

Similarly, Biden has shown determination to combat discrimination based on gender identification and sexual orientation. Soon after his election, he issued an executive order taking steps such as creating a White House Gender Policy Council to promote gender equity and equality. His administration has also displayed determination in promoting LGBT-Q rights by taking steps such as reversing a Trump-era regulation that discriminated against transgender army personnel. This outlook differs significantly from his predecessor, who was regularly accused of promoting gender bias and inequality.

It is also pertinent to mention that political analysts described President Trump's mishandling of the Covid-19 pandemic and the subsequent loss of lives as one of the most decisive factors for his failure in the 2020 elections. On the other hand, President Biden displayed intent on tackling the pandemic on a war front, taking steps to ensure SOPs, conducting mass-vaccination drives, and pushing for healthcare reforms. These efforts resulted in a drastic overall reduction of Covid-related deaths in the country.

On the other hand, President Trump's foreign policy, which was based on the idea of "America First", was decidedly isolationist. While many anti-interventionist political analysts have hailed this approach, others have criticized his decisions to exit from major international treaties and obligations such as the Iran Deal (JCPOA) and the Paris Climate Change agreement. The Biden administration's recent foreign policy statements and slogans such as "America is back" indicate a return to the internationalist realm, and it has recommitted to its climate change commitments. However, its stance on some important issues, such as Iran and North Korea, remains unclear.

While the Biden administration's agenda positively differs from Trump's in various regards, it is faced with many challenges - both on the foreign and domestic front. With regards to the former, among the most contentious issues is the United States' relationship with China, which has remained at an all-time low ever since the trade war that began in 2018. The economic tensions between the two countries are coupled with geopolitical tensions such as the issue of Taiwan or the Indian Ocean military-build up. While the United States needs to protect its economic and political interests, a confrontation with China is not viable. A mutual dialogue and diplomatic cooperation to restore trust between the two countries is a prerequisite for peace.

Similarly, amongst the Obama administration's major foreign policy successes was the historic JCPOA deal with Iran. While Trump withdrew from the agreement in 2018, pledging a "better deal", we are in the absence of any legal reassurance thus far. As a result, the ties between the United States and Iran have remained at an all-time low. The recent renegotiations over the nuclear deal in 2021 could be viewed with cautious optimism, as both countries seek to overcome their differences. However, several irritants, such as Iran's condition of removal of all sanctions, remain.

Other critical issues that need a decisive policy approach include the United States' attitude toward NATO in the aftermath of Trump's aggressive overtures and the broader Middle-East policy amidst the Israel-Palestine conflict and the Saudi-Iran tensions.

Conclusion

"The experience of democracy is like the experience
of life itself—always changing, infinite in its variety,
sometimes turbulent and all the more valuable for
having been tested in adversity"
—Jimmy Carter (1978)

With its roots sketching back to as early as the ancient Greek
period and its relevance being universal in the present world,
democracy could indeed be viewed as a dynamic, ever-evolving
political ideal that has continued to serve at the heart of politics
for over decades. As a quick recap, this book sought to provide an
overview of democracy's evolution over the different ages - from
the ancient Greek era, the Roman era, and the medieval era to
the twentieth-century and contemporary era. When we talk about
democracy's evolutionary character, we refer to the plethora of
legislative and institutional reforms in different periods and parts
of the world, which became permanent features of what we know
of democracy today.

The term "democracy" is derived from the Greek words "demos", meaning a citizen living within a particular state, and "kratos", i.e., power or authority. Besides the etymology, the Greeks introduced various democratic institutions, such as the vote, which revolved around politically empowering ordinary citizens of the city-state. The Roman Republic era further introduced and strengthened new democratic institutions such as the Senate and other legislative assemblies and the 'lot' system, to name a few. Similarly, several new institutions and democratic ideas were introduced in medieval-era England, which serve as cornerstones of politics today. Among these developments were the Magna Carta and the Bill of Rights, which served as a death blow to the theory of divine rights and paved the way for replacing monarchies worldwide with democratic government systems.

The development of democracy in the United States since its independence has also been analyzed in-depth in this book. Most of the American democratic institutions we see today, such as the bicameral congress, a presidential system, and the system of checks and balances, were established by the framers to forge a "stronger union" through an emphasis on federalism. With time, several constitutional amendments and new institutions were established, which made America "more democratic". The prominent examples of these include the abolishment of slavery and segregation in the 19th and 20th centuries, respectively, the right to vote for women, and a range of anti-gender discrimination laws.

Furthermore, the book also sought to analyze a series of developments in the twentieth century that led to America's rise as a significant world power and how this may have remained a myth without its well-functioning political system at home. Moreover, the period marked an internationalization of democracy in numerous ways, such as establishing international peace organizations like the United Nations and the World Trade Organisation.

We also sought to depict where democracy stands today by comparing and contrasting several countries that differ significantly in terms of their score on the democracy index. Our analysis suggests that while Nordic countries (Denmark, Finland, Iceland, Norway, and Sweden) have continued to secure top positions given their effective social welfare mechanisms, the United States of America has seen a sharp decline in its rankings, becoming a 'flawed democracy' since 2016. On the other hand, several countries that were previously hybrid regimes, such as India, have seen a recent deterioration in their rankings due to a multitude of factors, with the most prominent one being populistic politics. However, there are several success stories, such as Taiwan, where democracy and people's faith in their government and regime have strengthened over time. We also shed light on several countries that have remained the least democratic in their character. China, Russia, and the Gulf States are key examples of this.

Winston Churchill (1947) once famously remarked, "Indeed, it has been said that democracy is the worst form of government except all those other forms that have been tried from time to time." However, despite an overwhelming consensus about democracy as the most suitable system of government, democracy has arguably backtracked across the world in recent times. Therefore, we sought to explore some of the key factors that threaten democracy today, ranging from the rise of radical populism worldwide to institutional challenges such as corruption, red-tapism, gerrymandering, etc.

As Oscar Wilde suggests, "We are all in the gutter, but some of us are looking at the stars". While democracy has undoubtedly displayed signs of recession in recent times, one must remain optimistic about its future. It is important to note that while the American democracy may be flawed and exhibit its fault-lines, what makes it stand out is its resilience. Most Americans have outrightly rejected those who attempt to sow discord and polarisation, using the power of the vote and legal mechanisms. Similarly, other nations worldwide have expressed their strong desire for multilateral cooperation, human rights, and liberties - which serve as the fundamental principles of democracy.

Thank you for reading!

Thank you for your purchase. If you enjoyed this book, feel free to leave a review on Amazon. This will help us continue to provide great books, and it will help our potential buyers make confident buying decisions. We will be forever grateful - thank you in advance!

HTTPS://WWW.RPBOOK.CO.UK/AZR/B0B25R8R86

Also By Eric Nilsen:

Understanding Social Justice

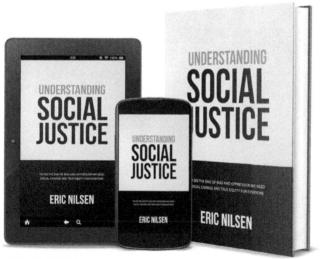

 HTTPS://MYBOOK.TO/SOCIALJUSTICE

Glossary

Autocracy: a form of government in which absolute power over a state is concentrated in the hands of one person, whose decisions are subject to no external legal constraints or will of the public.

Aristocracy: a form of government in which political power is wrested in the hands of a small, privileged ruling class.

Bicameral: a type of legislature that is divided into two separate assemblies, houses, or chambers.

Capitalism: a political and economic system in which private or individuals control a country's trade and industry.

Centrist: a political outlook that involves acceptance of social equality along with a degree of social hierarchy while resisting any radical changes that would shift the society to the right or the left.

Clause: a particular and separate article or provision in a legal document.

Corporatist: the organization of society by large groups who share a common interest or profession.

Cronyism: the practice of awarding political or administrative positions or privileges to friends or trusted colleagues, regardless of their qualifications.

Deductive Method: the process of reaching a conclusion based on premises generally considered true.

Democracy: a form of government in which power is vested in all citizens, who can elect their representatives directly or indirectly.

Executive: the branch of government responsible for putting legislation or laws into effect.

Filibustering: a political procedure/tactic used to obstruct the passage of legislation, commonly by speaking excessively.

Gerrymandering: a political procedure/tactic used to manipulate the boundaries of an electoral constituency to favor one political party over the other.

Guided Democracy (or managed democracy): a government which is formally democratic, but in reality functions as an authoritarian or autocratic government.

Guild Democracy: A medieval union of craftsmen or merchants wielding considerable political power to pursue similar goals.

Habeas Corpus: a legal process under which an individual who is unlawfully detained can be set free.

Hybrid Regime: a mixed political regime that is often created by an incomplete transition from an authoritarian regime into a democratic one.

Inductive Method: a type of reasoning in which general conclusions are drawn from a set of specific observations.

Isolationism: a national policy of avoiding political or economic connections with other countries, which may lead to conflict or war.

Judiciary: the branch of government that comprises of courts which are vested with judicial power.

Judicial Review: the power of courts to review executive, legislative and administrative actions of the government and declare them null and void if found unconstitutional.

Left-wing politics: a political outlook that supports social equality and egalitarianism, often in opposition to social hierarchy.

Legislation: the process of making or enacting laws by a legislature (such as the Congress in the case of U.S.A)

Legitimacy: the right and acceptance of an authority, such as a state or regime.

Liberalization: the loosening of government controls or relaxation of laws pertaining to economic or social matters.

Mandate: the authority given by the electorate to a party or politician that wins an election.

Monarchy: a form of government in which a single person is head of state for life until abdication. The monarch's right to rule is generally inherited.

Oligarchy: a form of government in which political power is vested in a small group of people.

Proportional representation: an electoral system with a representative body that reflects the overall distribution of voters' preference for a particular political party.

Progressivism: a political or social-reform movement aimed at addressing the interests of ordinary citizens through political action and reform.

Red Tapism: an idiom referring to excessive paperwork and conformity to official rules that hinders action or decision-making.

Right-wing politics: a political outlook that views certain social orders or hierarchies as inevitable or desirable, typically supporting this proposition based on religion, tradition or natural law.

Secularism: The separation of religion from state institutions and the public sphere.

Socialism: a political, economic or social philosophy which advocates that the means of production, exchange and distribution should be owned by the community as a whole.

Ultra Vires: an act done by an individual or institution which is beyond its legal power and authority.

Unicameral: a type of legislature that has a single legislative house or chamber.

Bibliography

Herman, A. (n.d.). *5 reasons why Plato and Aristotle still matter Today*. PublishersWeekly.com. Retrieved January 21, 2022, from https://www.publishersweekly.com/pw/by-topic/industry-news/tip-sheet/article/60264-5-reasons-why-plato-and-aristotle-still-matter-today.html

Australia, H. of R. (1931, July 17). *House of Representatives, debates, 17 July 1931 :: Historic Hansard*. Australia, House of Representatives. Retrieved January 21, 2022, from http://historichansard.net/hofreps/1931/19310717_reps_12_131/

Biswas, S. (2021, March 16). *'Electoral autocracy': The downgrading of India's democracy*. BBC News. Retrieved January 17, 2022, from https://www.bbc.com/news/world-asia-india-56393944

Briggs, P. J. (1969). *Congress and Collective Security: The Resolutions of 1943*. World Affs., 132, 332.

British Library. (n.d.). Retrieved January 21, 2022, from https://www.bl.uk/magna-carta/articles/the-origins-of-magna-carta

Brown, L. (1998). *How Totalitarian is Plato's Republic.* Essays on Plato's Republic, 13-27.

Brown, Z. S. (2016, November 1). *How democratic was the Roman Republic? The theory and practice of an archetypal democracy.* Inquiries Journal. Retrieved January 21, 2022, from http://www.inquiriesjournal.com/articles/1492/how-democratic -was-the-roman-republic-the-theory-and-practice-of-an-archetyp al-democracy

Challenges to democracy. Challenges to Democracy. (n.d.). Retrieved January 17, 2022, from https://scholar.harvard.edu/dziblatt/challenges-democracy

Coleman, T. (n.d.). *Three proposals to strengthen American democracy.* Institute of Politics and Global Affairs. Retrieved January 28, 2022, from https://iopga.cornell.edu/three-proposals-to-strengthen-america n-democracy/

Congress, U. S. (1776). *"Declaration of independence."* Available from http://memory. loc. gov/cgi-bin/ampage

Constitution, U. S. (1787). *"Preamble".* Available from http://www. house. gov/Constitution/Constitution. html

De Tocqueville, A. (1838). *Democracy in america.* London: Saunders and Otley.

Deutsche Welle. (n.d.). *Qatari elections: A PR stunt or a step toward democracy?: DW: 24.08.2021.* DW.COM. Retrieved January 21, 2022, from https://www.dw.com/en/qatari-elections-a-pr-stunt-or-a-step-to ward-democracy/a-58970500

Fidrmuc J. (2001, April 26). *Economic Reform, Democracy and Growth During Post-Communist Transition.* Available from https://papers.ssrn.com/sol3/papers.cfm?abstract_id=267275

Fisher, J. (2015, March 13). *Why Magna Carta still matters today.* British Library. Retrieved January 21, 2022, from https://www.bl.uk/magna-carta/articles/why-magna-carta-still-matters-today

Friedman, M. (1982). *Capitalism and Freedom.* 1962.

Gray, D. (2021, January 25). *UK at risk of becoming failed state, says Gordon Brown.* The Guardian. Retrieved January 21, 2022, f r o m https://www.theguardian.com/politics/2021/jan/25/uk-at-risk-of-becoming-failed-state-says-gordon-brown

Grinde Jr, D. A., & Johansen, B. E. (1991). *Exemplar of Liberty: Native America and the Evolution of Democracy.* Native American Politics Series No. 3.

Herman, A. (2013, December 6). *"5 Reasons Why Plato and Aristotle Still Matter Today".* PublishersWeekly.com. https://www.publishersweekly.com/pw/by-topic/industry-news/tip-sheet/article/60264-5-reasons-why-plato-and-aristotle-still-matter-today.html

Holt, J. C., Garnett, G., & Hudson, J. (2015). *Magna carta.* Cambridge University Press. Chicago

Møller, J. (2015, August 24). *Exploring the medieval roots of democracy and State Building in Europe.* EUROPP. Retrieved January 21, 2022, from https://blogs.lse.ac.uk/europpblog/2015/08/18/exploring-the-medieval-roots-of-democracy-and-state-building-in-europe/

Latham, J.G., Australia, H. of R. (1931, July 17). *House of Representatives, debates, 17 July 1931.* Historic Hansard. Australia, House of Representatives. Retrieved January 21, 2022, from http://historichansard.net/hofreps/1931/19310717_reps_12_131/

Jha, P. (2017). *How the BJP Wins: Inside India's Greatest Election Machine.* Juggernaut Books. Chicago

Kaminski, J. P. (Ed.). (1992). *The bill of rights and the states: the colonial and revolutionary origins of American liberties.* Rowman & Littlefield.

Li, G. (2021, February 4). *Taiwan leapfrogs Japan and South Korea to top asia democracy table.* Nikkei Asia. Retrieved January 21, 2022, from https://asia.nikkei.com/Politics/Taiwan-leapfrogs-Japan-and-South-Korea-to-top-Asia-democracy-table

Macalister, R. A. S. (1914). *The Philistines: their history and civilization.* British Academy. Chicago

Madison, J. (1787, November 22). *The federalist no. 10.*

Moore, M. (2021, July 25). *American optimism on direction of US plummets nearly 20 points: Poll.* New York Post. Retrieved January 21, 2022, from https://nypost.com/2021/07/25/american-optimism-on-direction-of-us-plummets/

Muhlberger, S. (1998). *Democracy in ancient India.* Chicago

Munro, C. (1999). *Studies in constitutional law.* Butterworths.

The New York Times (1978, January 3). *Text of address by President Carter before the Indian Parliament in New Delhi.* The New York Times. Retrieved January 17, 2022, from https://www.nytimes.com/1978/01/03/archives/text-of-address-by-president-carter-before-the-indian-parliament-in.html

Ogden, D. M., & Peterson, A. L. (1968). *Electing the President.* Chandler Publishing Company.

Peev, E., & Mueller, D. C. (2012). *Democracy, economic freedom and growth in transition economies.* Kyklos, 65(3), 371-407.

Reeve, C. D. (2004). *Plato: Republic.* Hackett, Indianapolis. Chicago

Rhodes, P. J. (2007). *The Greek city states: A source book.* Cambridge University Press.

Stalley, R. F. (Ed.). (1998). *The politics.* Oxford Paperbacks.

Rogoff, K. (2016, June 24). *Britain's democratic failure* . Project Syndicate. Retrieved January 21, 2022, from https://www.project-syndicate.org/commentary/brexit-democratic-failure-for-uk-by-kenneth-rogoff-2016-06

Swann, S., et al. (2021, October 6). *United States ranks 25th in latest democracy index.* The Fulcrum. Retrieved January 17, 2022, f r o m https://thefulcrum.us/big-picture/the-economist-democracy-index

National Archives and Records Administration (n.d.). *The bill of rights: What does it say?* Retrieved January 21, 2022, from https://www.archives.gov/founding-docs/bill-of-rights/what-does-it-say#:~:text=The%20Bill%20of%20Rights%20is%20the%20first%2010%20Amendments%20to%20the%20Constitution.&text=It%20guarantees%20civil%20rights%20and,the%20people%20or%20the%20States

The Economist Intelligence Unit (n.d.). *EIU Democracy Index 2019 - World Democracy Report.* Retrieved January 17, 2022, from https://www.eiu.com/topic/democracy-index/

International Churchill Society (1947, November 11). *The worst form of Government.* Retrieved January 21, 2022, from https://winstonchurchill.org/resources/quotes/the-worst-form-of-government/

Titlestad, T. (2020). *Alexandra Sanmark, Viking Law and Order: Places and Rituals of Assembly in the Medieval North.* Available from https://www.euppublishing.com/doi/full/10.3366/nor.2020.0206

Watts, E. J. (2021). *The eternal decline and fall of Rome: the history of a dangerous idea.* Oxford University Press.

Wilson, W. (1918). *Wilson's Fourteen Points.* Woodrow Wilson Presidential Library. Retrieved December 5, 2007.

Zhu, Y. (2011). *"Performance legitimacy" and China's political adaptation strategy.* Journal of Chinese Political Science, 16(2).

Ziblatt, D. (n.d.). *Challenges to democracy.* Challenges to Democracy. Retrieved January 21, 2022, from https://scholar.harvard.edu/dziblatt/challenges-democracy

Made in the USA
Middletown, DE
14 August 2023

36705845R00076